BEST RADIO
PLAYS OF 1982

BEST RADIO PLAYS OF 1982

The Giles Cooper Award Winners

Rhys Adrian: Watching the Plays Together
John Arden: The Old Man Sleeps Alone
Harry Barton: Hoopoe Day
Donald Chapman: Invisible Writing
Tom Stoppard: The Dog It Was That Died
(*by arrangement with Faber and Faber*)
William Trevor: Autumn Sunshine

METHUEN/BBC PUBLICATIONS

First published in Great Britain in 1983 by Methuen London Ltd,
11 New Fetter Lane, London EC4P 4EE and BBC Publications,
35 Marylebone High Street, London W1M 4AA.

Set in IBM 10 point Journal by 𝓕\ Tek-Art, Croydon, Surrey
Printed in Great Britain by Richard Clay (The Chaucer Press) Ltd,
Bungay, Suffolk

ISBN 0 413 52540 6

CONTENTS

THE GILES COOPER AWARDS: a note on the selection

Giles Cooper

As one of the most original and inventive radio playwrights of the post-war years, Giles Cooper was the author that came most clearly to mind when the BBC and Methuen were in search of a name when first setting up their jointly sponsored radio drama awards in 1978. Particularly so, as the aim of the awards is precisely to encourage original radio writing by both new and established authors — encouragement in the form both of public acclaim and of publication of their work in book form.

Eligibility

Eligible for the awards was every original radio play first broadcast by the BBC domestic service from December 1981 to December 1982 (almost 500 plays in total). Excluded from consideration were translations, adaptations and dramatised 'features'. In order to ensure that the broad range of radio playwriting was represented, the judges aimed to select plays which offered a variety of length, subject matter and technique by authors with differing experience of writing for radio.

Selection

The producers-in-charge of the various drama 'slots' were each asked to put forward about five or six plays for the judges' consideration. This resulted in a 'short-list' of some 30 plays from which the final selection was made. The judges were entitled to nominate further plays for consideration provided they were eligible. Selection was made on the strength of the script rather than of the production, since it was felt that the awards were primarily for *writing* and that production could unduly enhance or detract from the merits of the original script.

Judges

The judges for the 1982 awards were:
 Martin Esslin, Professor of Drama, Stanford University, California and ex-head of BBC Radio Drama
 Nicholas Hern, Drama Editor, Methuen London
 Richard Imison, Script Editor, BBC Radio Drama
 Gillian Reynolds, radio critic, *The Daily Telegraph*

PREFACE

Britain is the centre of the world for radio drama, and yet, if you were to consider writing a history of British awards for creative achievement in radio, it would become rapidly apparent not merely that the volume would be a slim one but that most single attempts to recognise and celebrate the best of radio in this country have been almost as ephemeral as the medium itself.

That's a shame, and it's also somewhat surprising, given the range and quality of material that has been broadcast over the years, together with the talent and enthusiasm of those involved in creating it, the support of such influential bodies as the Society of Authors and the Writers Guild of Great Britain, and — by no means least important — the availability of commercial sponsorship.

From time to time, the combined efforts of several of the above have led to the establishment of a new award, or the inclusion of Radio as a category in an existing scheme; juries and systems of nomination have been devised, ceremonies stage-managed and trophies designed, in order to provide writers, producers and performers with a more lasting tribute to their success. Yet all of them, after a very few years, have either ceased to exist or have changed so radically that it is hard even for the professional observer to recognise the tangible symbol, let alone the underlying principles, of consecutive awards.

Yet at the heart of a meaningful award is continuity: of purpose, of method and indeed of outward show. One can hardly imagine the Oscar achieving its historic status in the world of film if at intervals it had changed its now celebrated shape, let alone its name, method of choosing finalists, and presentation ceremony. It is the knowledge of those who over the years have shared in the same sequence of nomination, suspense and final selection that gives the award such special prestige, as well no doubt as guiding the members of the Academy. A similar historical sense guides the international juries of the Prix Italia, an event at which professional prizes have been given to outstanding radio and television programmes for more than thirty-five years.

When the Giles Cooper Awards were first conceived in 1978, they were seen as an addition to other national prizes which were then available. It was in the minds of those of us who were involved that radio, a writers' medium before all else, should have an award solely for writers and that those who nominated for the award should be the editors and producers who were continuously employed in the business of radio play selection and production. It was of the essence that it should be an award from fellow professionals and that its public expression should be rescue from the fate of that evanescence to which most radio is doomed, by publication in a collected volume of the year.

The task that faced the first panel of judges was no light one. In 1978, BBC Radio's domestic services had broadcast over 450 original radio plays, of widely varying style and subject matter, and ranging from thirty minutes to more than two hours in length. Even after the narrowing of choice by nomination and shortlisting, the panel was considering the equivalent of almost one play a week throughout the year and their final selection reflected the fact that the Radio Drama Department runs not one theatre, but several, each catering for different expectations and clientele.

What was remarkable in 1978 has grown even more remarkable in the ensuing five years, although sadly it has become even more exceptional in world broadcasting terms. The 450 radio plays have become over 500 and there have also been expansions of the form in both experimental and popular drama. On the one hand, the clearly definable radio play and the imaginative feature have moved closer together so that it is, at the extreme, increasingly hard to categorise a particular work; on the other hand there has been a sharp increase in demand for the conventionally shaped narrative in the traditions of the classic thriller or comedy. In between, all kinds of radio writing are acceptable, and most are being offered, though there has been for some years a tendency on the part of writers to avoid areas of poetic imagination in which the medium is traditionally strong.

Perhaps this last point simply reflects a change in preoccupation among dramatists in general. Certainly, it is true that there has been a move towards drama of greater contemporary political and social realism; also, there has been wider realisation in all parts of the output that at the heart of much good radio drama is simply dialogue so structured as to provoke the most vivid mental pictures; the kind of play which on the page looks deceptively simple, eschews obvious radiophonics but which actually exploits the strength of the medium with precision and assurance.

The past year has, unhappily, seen a weakening of radio drama's role in some parts of the world. Increasing economic pressure, combined in certain instances with a failure of confidence on the part of broadcasters in their creative role, has led to cutbacks and reallocation of resources. Radio drama, though almost immeasurably cheaper than its television counterpart, is nevertheless expensive in radio terms — and therefore vulnerable at times of financial crisis. In Australia, and in both Canada and the United States, it now plays a very small part in the radio output as a whole. Even in some European countries, where the drama tradition was stronger, there have been moves to reduce both the length and number of individual plays.

In the face of this, the British achievement calls for some analysis. Undoubtedly, it reflects the quite extraordinarily high level of creative activity amongst both professional and part-time writers. Without such wells of talent to draw on, so large an output would soon cease to flourish. It reflects, too, I believe, the very strong tradition within the BBC itself which sustains belief in the role of demanding and creative radio alongside other forms of public service. Most of all, it reflects the encouragement and response of an audience, measured in comfortably large figures, which seldom allows for complacency over individual achievements but repeatedly makes it clear that ideal radio drama is not only conceivable but achievable, and should be striven for. That's the best kind of support.

As I write, some new awards for radio have just been established and are due to be deliberated and presented in the course of 1983. Like their predecessors, they are welcome; may they live long enough to acquire stature. Meanwhile, in this, their fifth year, the Giles Cooper Awards have gone, we think, to a collection of plays whose merit is evident upon the page. They were all hard pressed, in a year which contained the BBC's 60th Anniversary commissions, in addition to much else that was excellent in radio writing. Together, they form a challenge to the writers of 1983, which they — and we — should be eager to take up.

Richard Imison
(February 1983)

WATCHING THE PLAYS TOGETHER

by Rhys Adrian

For Marianne de Barde

Rhys Adrian was born in London and lives and works in Chiswick. He was a stage manager for summer shows, revues, pantomimes and West End musicals before becoming a full-time writer. He is married to dancer Mavis Traill and has two sons.

Watching the Plays Together was first broadcast on BBC Radio 3 on 17th October 1982. The cast was as follows:

ROSEMARY	Rosemary Leach
GERALD	James Grout
DOCTOR	Ronald Herdman
WOMAN	Frances Jeater

Director: John Tydeman

Sporadic muted sounds of a TV programme in the background from time to time.

ROSEMARY. I always hate it when a play I am watching makes me feel guilty.

GERALD. Does the play we are now watching make you feel guilty?

ROSEMARY. I don't know. Not yet.

GERALD. But you never watch a play. You always talk all the way through a play. Each play you watch you talk all the way through it. Sometimes you leave the room for minutes on end when you watch a play. What does this play make you feel?

ROSEMARY. I don't know. Not yet. Well. Uneasy.

GERALD. The dramatist has stumbled upon some immutable truth. That after a while relationships have a tendency to decay and to wither away. As a general rule. Something that has been known to the rest of us since we first started to form relationships of our own. The decay from within. The seeds of which were there from the very beginning. But he has stumbled across it, almost in the dark, a flash, a blinding revelation, then we have to sit here and endure it, while he imposes the bleakness of his own view upon the rest of us.

ROSEMARY. But you don't like a play at all. You don't like any kind of play.

GERALD. I've never liked a play. I've never seen the point in liking a play. It is easier to like a dog or a cat than to like a play. A play cannot like you back. So what is the point in liking it? What is the point in liking something that cannot like you back?

ROSEMARY. You like your pipe.

GERALD. I don't like my pipe. I smoke my pipe.

ROSEMARY. It's the same thing.

GERALD. Liking is a two way process. To like one has to be liked in return. It is like saying that one likes this brand of soap. Or that packet of detergent. How can one like a particular brand of detergent?

ROSEMARY. I'm rather fond of the brand I use.

GERALD. But the brand you use is just like any other brand. The content is the same. Only the packet is different.

ROSEMARY. But all the plays are different.

GERALD. A lot of them seem the same to me. The same ideas. The same faces. The same old twaddle.

ROSEMARY. You don't like a play because you don't like being taken out of yourself.

GERALD. Why should I want to be taken out of myself? I am perfectly content to remain where I am. Within myself.

ROSEMARY. But the author can take you out of your world and into his.

GERALD. But the world he depicts is often one of extreme squalor. Why should I want to be taken out of my world and into his? We don't live in conditions of squalor.

ROSEMARY. Frightened the author might say something you might not like? Something that might touch on a raw nerve.

GERALD. You mean some vile truth that has been known to us all along? He can say what he likes. As long as he doesn't expect me to be moved by it. Or to be affected in any way.

ROSEMARY. Not all the plays are squalid.

GERALD. The one we are now watching is. It's extremely squalid.

ROSEMARY. But we don't know that, do we? We're not watching it. We're talking all the way through it.

GERALD. You started to talk. I was watching the play.

ROSEMARY. You were doing your crossword.

GERALD. I was doing my crossword as well as watching the play. Are we to sit here and applaud the squalor of the scene he depicts? The filthy children. The inadequate mother. The feckless husband. The appalling room they all seem to be living in. The filthy conditions?

ROSEMARY. It's a play about the socially deprived.

GERALD. That may be how you see it. And you suggest that I should be glad to escape from my world into his?

ROSEMARY. It's been written by a woman.

GERALD. Man. Woman. What's the difference?

ROSEMARY. It makes a lot of difference.

GERALD. How?

ROSEMARY. Well . . . it's always interesting to follow the work of a particular author.

GERALD. How is it interesting?

ROSEMARY. I don't suppose you even know who's written it.

GERALD. And what difference would it make to my enjoyment of it if I did?

ROSEMARY. Then you don't know!

GERALD. Why should I?

ROSEMARY. You see! You don't even know who's written it!

GERALD. Do you? (*Pause*.) Well? Do you?

ROSEMARY. Well. Yes. I did.

GERALD. Then who did write it?

ROSEMARY. Well. The name escapes me for the minute. But I did know. I knew before the play began. I took the trouble to look it up. (*Pause*.) You are taken out of yourself.

GERALD. Have you been taken out of yourself? Now. This minute. As far as I can see you are still seated in that chair. You seem very much within yourself to me.

ROSEMARY. All I'm saying is that an author can sometimes take you over. Can sometimes take you out of yourself.

GERALD. But I have no wish to be taken over. I have no wish to be taken out of myself. I prefer to remain firmly fixed within myself. I have my own anxieties to contend with. I have no wish to share in the anxiety of others. I've sampled all the arts at one time or another. Words scattered about the page. Daubs of paint on canvas.

ROSEMARY. But a good play can make you more understanding. More caring.

GERALD. But I don't want to understand the play we are watching. I don't want a more caring attitude to the world he depicts. And, anyway, how do we know the world he depicts has a grain of truth in it? They are just actors. They have learned their lines. They have been moved around like puppets by the director. The dirt has been painted onto the faces of the children. There is twelve minutes of the play to go. Twelve minutes for the play to resolve itself. He was beastly to her. She has been beastly back to him. I don't like him. And I don't like her. I didn't like the ghastly children. I didn't like the awful mother. I don't much care for the situation they have found themselves in. I haven't minded in the least that the authorities have been shown as a group of uncaring individuals. That seems to me, so far, to have been the only point in its favour. They are supposed to be poor yet they can afford to smoke incessantly and watch the television all day long. An incredible amount of alcohol consumed. He seemed never to be out of the pub. It seems a very poor representation of life too. It is all water off a duck's back to me. I have sat here for the past hour not liking any of it. But I have done my crossword. So something has been achieved. It has helped me concentrate on that.

ROSEMARY. Then you can't have taken anything from it at all.

GERALD. Taken anything from what?

ROSEMARY. The play. (*Pause.*) Anyway, it's not a very good play.

GERALD. Then why have we been watching it?

ROSEMARY. I like a play.

GERALD. You don't seem to like this one.

ROSEMARY. How do you know whether you are going to like a play or not until you have seen it?

GERALD. But you surely don't want to be taken out of this world into that world? His world.

ROSEMARY. It's her world. It's written from the woman's point of view.

GERALD. You left the room for a good ten minutes during the course of it.

ROSEMARY. I went to make some tea. Besides. There was a lull coming up.

GERALD. A lull?

ROSEMARY. A lull in the play. I can always tell when there's one coming up. It is the author getting his second wind. It is the author taking a pause. It is the author taking stock of his situation and trying to fix his sights again.

GERALD. He has been floundering in a lull of one kind or another since he began it.

ROSEMARY. There was the quarrel.

GERALD. I didn't pay any attention to it.

ROSEMARY. There was the moment when the authorities tried to evict them.

GERALD. A pity they didn't.

ROSEMARY. There was the social worker who took up the case for them.

GERALD. Seen it all before.

ROSEMARY. Anyway. I don't suppose anything happened.

GERALD. When?

ROSEMARY. During the lull. While I was making the tea.

GERALD. I wouldn't know. I switched channels when you were out of the room. There didn't seem to be much going on there either.

Pause.

ROSEMARY. I watched a play the other day. There was an actor in it. Someone like you. He seemed to think like you. He spoke like you. He didn't like a play either. He smoked a pipe too.

GERALD. Was he watching a play too?

ROSEMARY. They both were. He and the wife. That was the point of it. It was all fearfully well done. Until about half way through the author suddenly seemed to lose all sight of where he was going. They talked all the way through the play they were watching too. From time to time the woman would leave the room to make some tea. That was the play. And the play they were watching was about people watching a play. It was meant to point up the irony of the situation they were soon to find themselves in, do you see?

GERALD. Was there any humour in it?

ROSEMARY. It wasn't a humorous play. It was just that the play, the play they were watching, well, seemed to strike some chord or other in them.

GERALD. The people in the play?

ROSEMARY. Yes.

GERALD. The people in the play watching the play within the play?

ROSEMARY. Yes.

GERALD. Not the people within the play they were watching.

ROSEMARY. It was what they said. I think. The people in the play they were watching. But the people in the play watching the play within the play ended up having the most fearful quarrel because of it.

GERALD. They ended up hating each other?

ROSEMARY. Yes.

GERALD. All because they'd watched this play?

ROSEMARY. Yes. But it came out that they'd hated each other underneath all along. The people watching the play, but hadn't realised it until they watched the play within the play which somehow seemed to lay bare the waste of their own lives to them, do you see? They'd thought they'd just been sitting there having a cup of tea and watching a play. They hadn't realised what they were in for. Otherwise they wouldn't have watched. It was the wife, do you see? She wanted to watch the play. She always liked a play. He couldn't have cared whether he watched a play or not. But up until then, when the play gave them each such a slap in the face, they'd always thought they'd got on tolerably well with each other. Until that moment, in the play that sparked it all off. But it seemed that over the years they'd barely tolerated each other at all. Putting up with each other's foibles. Putting up with each other's bad habits. He'd never been able to stand her cooking. Always wanted to be violently sick, do you see, after one of her meals. His coughing kept her awake all night. Cough, cough, cough, all night long, was what she said. She never slept. All sorts of things like that.

GERALD. And they ended up realising how much they'd hated each other all those years. After the play?

ROSEMARY. It was during the play. It was during the play that they were watching that they had the most fearful quarrel.

GERALD. And this play, the play within the play, was what gave them this insight into their own lives?

ROSEMARY. A glimpse into hell was how one of them put it. You saw it too.

GERALD. How did it end?

ROSEMARY. I don't know. The phone rang. It was Mother. She'd been watching the play too. She said she found it too disturbing. Could hardly bear to go on watching it. She said it put her in mind of Father.

GERALD. And this is what is meant by being taken out of one's self. To have the waste of one's own life laid bare to one's self. To have one's pitiful inadequacies held up for all to see.

ROSEMARY. It was only a play. And they were only actors. It was just that watching the play within the play that sparked it all off. It was all fearfully well done.

GERALD. And this play put you in mind of me?

ROSEMARY. Not the play I was watching. The play they were watching.

GERALD. And were the people in the play within the play quarrelling in the same way that the people watching the play were quarrelling?

ROSEMARY. They weren't quarrelling at all.

GERALD. Then what was it that sparked off this sudden realisation?

ROSEMARY. It wasn't so much sparked off as gradually revealed to them. They began to realise the truth of their own feelings for each other as they were watching the play. It was all very gradual.

GERALD. But didn't they know they'd hated each other. Until they saw the play?

ROSEMARY. They'd known all the time. It was just that over the years they'd suppressed their true feelings for each other. It was all fearfully well done. Until he lost sight of where he was going.

GERALD. Who?

ROSEMARY. The author.

GERALD. And what was the play about? The one they were watching? The actors?

ROSEMARY. Hard to say. They didn't let you see much of the play they were watching.

GERALD. Then what was it that sparked it all off?

ROSEMARY. It was a sort of love story. The play the actors were watching. It was about two people falling in love. Against the most fearful odds. Both families were dead against it, do you see. The girl's family didn't think much of the man and the man's family didn't think anything at all of the girl. It was set between the wars. They were terribly poor. It was the depression. Well, the woman who was watching the play within the play said to the actor who was with her that it reminded her of their early days. Their early struggles. Well the actor who was watching the play with her didn't like that one bit and they moved the camera closer to his face and you saw his upper lip start to quiver. It was as if he didn't want to be reminded of those early years, the early struggles, the barren years to come. He didn't want to be reminded in the least bit that he'd once been in love with the woman who was sitting next to him, do you see. He got into the most fearful rage. He had quite a job to hold back the tears. He became almost apoplectic with rage. He did it most fearfully well. He started to knead the cushion. She became tearful and they had the most fearful quarrel. Then he became short of breath. Then he stood up and then he collapsed back into the chair. It was really quite dramatic. Really riveting stuff. Then they called the doctor who said he'd had a coronary. And they took him off to intensive care where they battled to save his life, where you suspected all along that he didn't want to be brought out of his coma, do you see, that he just wanted to end it all there and then, but eventually they got him round. She didn't go near the hospital. She couldn't. Not after all the things they'd said to each other. She spent most of the rest of the time on the phone to her mother. Then, when he got better, while he was in hospital he'd had time to reflect on things, do you see. And there was quite a pretty nurse he was able to confide in. So when he was finally discharged he decided he didn't want to return to his former way of life so he got a room in a lodging house and went to live on his own. Then there was the divorce. And in the end she was left in the house on her own watching the plays and he was left on his own in his room staring at the four walls. Then he took to the bottle. She ended up taking masses of Valium. It all ended up in the most fearful squalor. It seemed a pretty poor resolution to me. All sorts of things left up in the air. A feeling that the author had cheated somehow. It all ended in the bleakest possible way. I wasn't sure how we were meant to react. No uplift. No solution. No real conclusion. No light at the end of the tunnel at all. Pretty poor stuff all round, I thought.

GERALD. And that was the end of it?

ROSEMARY. What I saw of it.

GERALD. But I thought you said you didn't see the end?

ROSEMARY. I watched the end while I was on the phone talking to Mother.

GERALD. And did she see the end while she was on the phone talking to you?

ROSEMARY. I suppose so. She didn't say. But I expect she did.

GERALD. Then you did see the whole play.

ROSEMARY. You did too.

GERALD. I don't remember any of it.

ROSEMARY. Well. I suppose I saw some of it. Well. Not all of it. I was in and out of the room quite a bit.

GERALD. I've never known you to watch a play right the way through.

ROSEMARY. I like a play that's true to life.

GERALD. But none of them are true to life. They are all made up.

ROSEMARY. I like a play where you feel the actor knows exactly what he's doing. That he knows exactly where he's going.

GERALD. The actors learn their lines and once having learned them and said them they then go home and forget them. Besides. You always leave the room during the course of a play and go and make yourself a cup of tea.

ROSEMARY. Only when there's a lull coming up.

GERALD. Sometimes you don't even see the ends to plays. Sometimes the play has ended before you even come back into the room. Or your mother is on the phone.

ROSEMARY. I've never seen you watch a play.

GERALD. I always do watch them.

ROSEMARY. You always do your crossword while they're on.

GERALD. I never leave the room. I see the plays all the way through. Even if, sometimes, it means hanging on to the bitter end.

ROSEMARY. You don't have to watch them just because I watch them.

GERALD. This is the living-room.

ROSEMARY. You could potter about. There are always plenty of things to do about the house.

GERALD. I don't want to potter about. After dinner I want to be able to put my feet up and relax. You don't take anything of it in, do you?

ROSEMARY. What do you mean?

GERALD. The plays you watch.

ROSEMARY. Well . . . there was that play the other day.

GERALD. Which play was that?

ROSEMARY. It was one of those about the changing face of Britain. It was the one where the author got himself into the most frightful muddle. It was the one about the coloureds who had just moved into the street. About the petition. About the role of police in society. That one.

GERALD. I don't remember seeing it.

ROSEMARY. You were watching it.

GERALD. Who was in it?

ROSEMARY. I don't remember who was in it. There was that blonde girl. The one who seems to be cropping up in everything these days. That rabbity middle-aged man. The one with the chip on his shoulder. Always plays the same part. It was about the sudden collapse of property values. With these people who had just moved into the street, do you see, the value of the properties came tumbling down. That one.

GERALD. I didn't see that one.

ROSEMARY. It was the one about the blight that had suddenly descended upon the street. It was as though the plague had suddenly arrived. Everyone up in arms about it. It was about living in a more caring society. That one.

GERALD. I don't remember anything of it.

ROSEMARY. Of course you saw it. It couldn't have sunk in, that's all. It really was most extraordinary.

GERALD. The play?

ROSEMARY. No. Mother. She called.

GERALD. She always calls after a play has been on.

ROSEMARY. This was the next day. She doesn't always call just when a play has been on.

GERALD. She always does.

ROSEMARY. She calls at other times as well. She calls at least six times a week. She likes to keep in touch. It hasn't been the same for her since Father died.

GERALD. Then what was so extraordinary about her calling?

ROSEMARY. It was the play. It seems that some friends of hers had been watching the play too. And they'd just had coloureds move into their street too. And the play had held up a mirror to their own predicament, do you see. But it hadn't shown a way out. As Mother said, it's all very well doing plays about the changing face of Britain but that the author could at least do something to show us a way out of the predicament we're all in. But it all ended up in the air, do you see. No hope. No way out. He just couldn't face up to it.

GERALD. Who?

ROSEMARY. Her husband.

GERALD. The husband in the play?

ROSEMARY. No. The husband of this friend of Mother's who was watching the play that we were watching. The one that Mother was watching too. Well what she saw of it. She was in and out of the room quite a bit during that one, she said. There was a lull of at least fifteen minutes while he seemed to be making up his mind and then he came to no obvious solution to it all. No solution. No conclusion. No uplift of any kind. Nothing at all in it to raise the spirits. Mother was very upset.

GERALD. How could she be upset. If she only saw bits of it?

ROSEMARY. She was upset because of her friend. It was the bitter truth of it, do you see. The coloureds had moved into their street too. Right across the street from them. Their living-room faced the street, do you see. They could see everything that went on. All the comings and goings.

GERALD. The actors in the play?

ROSEMARY. No. This friend of Mother's. The husband. The same thing had happened to them do you see. The way the play went on, it seemed to mock them, do you see. It held out no hope. No solution.

GERALD. Then what was so extraordinary about it?

ROSEMARY. The husband died.

GERALD. The husband in the play?

ROSEMARY. No. The husband of Mother's friend. It was while he was watching the play. According to Mother he had a coronary. He couldn't face up to it, do you see. The author had hit upon the idea of showing him his own predicament but hadn't shown him a way out. An awful raw nerve the author had hit upon. It gave him an awful jolt. An awful slap in the face. All that Mother sees are all the old values being eroded, do you see. All the old virtues. She hardly leaves the house at all now. Hardly dares to look out of the front windows. Never answers the door. Dreads the postman coming.

GERALD. Perhaps she oughtn't to watch the plays.

ROSEMARY. She likes to watch them. She likes a play that's true to life.

GERALD. And I am supposed to have seen this play?

ROSEMARY. You must remember.

GERALD. And you say you saw it?

ROSEMARY. Well. Bits of it.

GERALD. And how did it conclude?

ROSEMARY. I don't know. Of course we could all see what he was getting at right from the start. The most vile attack on the police. A really quite subversive piece. Undermining all decent standards. All the old virtues. Then when he started going over the same old ground for the umpteenth time, I could see it wasn't going to get anywhere, and then the most awful lull came up so I went out to the kitchen and peeled some potatoes. They seemed to write it up quite well in the paper, but I don't think he could have seen the play that I saw. He seemed to be writing about something quite different.

GERALD. Who?

ROSEMARY. Whoever wrote it up.

GERALD. Perhaps he was drunk.

ROSEMARY. Not in the play.

GERALD. The critic. Did he tell you how it ended?

ROSEMARY. No. Mother did.

GERALD. Then how did it end?

ROSEMARY. I don't remember.

GERALD. But if your mother saw the end and told you then you ought to know. I would have thought.

ROSEMARY. She said she stuck it out for as long as she could but she couldn't see the point in it. She thought it was awfully poor.

GERALD. But her friend saw the end?

ROSEMARY. Not according to Mother. Her husband died. She had all sorts of things to do. She did call Mother and ask her how it ended.

Pause.

GERALD. And the actor within the play of the first play you mentioned. He reminded you of me?

ROSEMARY. Just for the moment. Just the glimpse they gave us of him.

GERALD. There. The end. The play has come to an end and we have seen none of it.

ROSEMARY. I don't think I wanted to see the end to this one. The characters seemed the most frightful cut-outs to me. Awfully poor, I thought.

GERALD. But you saw none of it.

ROSEMARY. I saw all I needed to see of it.

The telephone rings.

Mother! . . . Yes. We've been watching it too. Awfully poor, we thought . . . You did too? And now you're watching the last part of the play on the other side . . . And there's the most awful lull. . . . And that's why you phoned. Mother, if you haven't seen the beginning of it then perhaps you oughtn't see the end. You might find it upsetting . . . I know you find most of them upsetting. But you think you'll stick it out till the end . . . You think it might pick up . . . Yes. Of course . . . We'll see you on Sunday. . . . We'll take you out for a drive.

She puts down the telephone.

That was Mother. She'd been watching the play too. She thought it was awfully poor. What she saw of it. She said she was in and out of the room quite a bit. And then someone called and tried to sell her something. She said she counted three lulls. Two quite short ones and one quite long. She thought he'd started out with no clear idea of where he was going and ended up with no clear idea of where he'd been.

GERALD. Who did?

ROSEMARY. The author.

GERALD. I thought you said it was a woman who wrote the play.

ROSEMARY. I don't see that it matters.

GERALD. It seemed to matter to you earlier on.

ROSEMARY. You're either going to get it from the man's point of view. Or you're going to get it from the woman's point of view. And you're going to watch it from your own point of view. So I don't see it matters in the least. All that matters is, that you watch it.

GERALD. Don't switch over. I want to see the news.

ROSEMARY. We saw the news earlier. It won't have changed much since then. Mother was right. There is a lull. I expect there's been the most fearful quarrel. She lying in bed gazing up at the ceiling. He lying in bed staring up at the ceiling. Acres of space between them. Both smoking.

From the TV set comes the sound of a police siren, very faint and receding.

GERALD. It's not the one about Ulster. The curtains aren't torn. The windows aren't broken.

ROSEMARY. In a moment I expect a child will cry and she will get up and cross the room, without a stitch on as likely as not.

GERALD. Perhaps it's about redundancy.

ROSEMARY. Perhaps the factory is about to close down. Perhaps there'll be a sit-in.

GERALD. Perhaps he's not the husband.

ROSEMARY. Perhaps she's drawing the social security for herself and the child and he shouldn't be there at all.

GERALD. Perhaps they're both drawing the social security and he's got a job on the side.

ROSEMARY. Well it's not the one about the anorexic living in the high rise flats. She's much too plump.

GERALD. Perhaps they're squatters. Perhaps it's a commune.

ROSEMARY. They can't be squatters. Squatters don't have beds.

GERALD. I do an arduous job. Eight hours a day. Two hours travelling. That's a ten hour day. Who's the mug? They are on social security. Plenty of money to spend. In and out of the pub all day long. Smoke incessantly. Cigarettes never out of their mouths. Watch the TV all day long. I don't see the point in seeking confirmation of one's own anxieties in a play.

ROSEMARY. But you have nothing to be anxious about. You have a nice home. Nice job. Nice car. I have a nice home. Nice job. Nice car. You're right. A play should take you over and take you out of yourself.

GERALD. But I didn't say that. You said that. I would be quite happy never to see another play. I hate watching the plays. A play often has the tendency to creep up on you and take you by surprise.

ROSEMARY. But that's the whole fun of them!

GERALD. But I don't want to be taken by surprise. I don't want to be sitting here and suddenly find myself getting a slap in the face. I don't want to be sitting here and quite suddenly find myself getting a ticking off during the course of it. You see. He hasn't put the cigarette out.

ROSEMARY. Perhaps he'll set fire to the bed. Perhaps that's the point of it. It's very much like the one, the one about the squatters and the commune, everyone on about human rights, that one, complete squalor, utter filth, where the child started to cry and before you knew where you were the entire house was in flames. Completely unwashed. Never went near a bath. That one. Mother thought it was very subversive. Not in the least bit life-like, she said. You see. They're quite close to each other now. While they were awake they were acres apart and now that they're asleep they're perfectly capable of reaching out and touching each other. Perhaps that's what they mean by it.

GERALD. None of it makes any sense to me.

ROSEMARY. But that's what you say about all of the plays.

GERALD. It's what I feel about most of them.

ROSEMARY. Finish your crossword.

GERALD. I've finished it.

ROSEMARY. Go to bed.

GERALD. I don't want to go to bed. Why should I go to bed just because I don't happen to like what I'm watching? (*Pause*.) Do you ever catch a glimpse of yourself?

ROSEMARY. Where?

GERALD. There. On the screen.

ROSEMARY. Sometimes. Do you?

GERALD. Sometimes.

ROSEMARY. In the plays?

GERALD. Not in the plays. The plays don't seem to take too kindly to people of my generation.

ROSEMARY. As you once were?

GERALD. Yes. And you?

ROSEMARY. As I once was. Yes. Not as I am now. I sometimes get a glimpse of myself when I'm watching an old movie. A glimpse of the past. As it was then. As I was. The old movies often give you a glimpse of what it was once like.

GERALD. I don't think I'd care to see a representation of myself. Not in a play. Not as a figment of someone else's imagination. I don't think I'd like that at all.

ROSEMARY. But if you saw someone who you thought was a representation of yourself then someone else might not think it was in the least bit like you. They might think that a representation of yourself that you didn't think was in the least bit like was more like you than you'd possibly care to admit.

Pause.

GERALD. Someone sometimes appears and I catch in them a glimpse of some toad at the office. Then I go into the office and I ask one of the toads if he'd seen the toad represented on the screen the night before and he says, Ho, Ho, Ho, and wasn't it like one of the toads we've got here. Completely missing the point, do you see. What is the point in some vile truth being expressed about you if you completely miss the point of it?

ROSEMARY. That's what I said.

GERALD. I have him fixed inside my head as the perfect toad and he has someone fixed inside his head as the perfect toad.

ROSEMARY. But he saw the same character portrayed as you did. Was this a play?

GERALD. I don't know what it was. I'd come into the room looking for something. The thing was on. I only caught a glimpse of what was happening. He said he'd only caught a glimpse of it. He'd come into the room while the thing was on. He'd come into the room looking for something too. He caught a glimpse of this toad-like creature and he said to his wife, if he said anything at all to his wife, that the toad-like creature he'd caught a glimpse of reminded him of one of the toads at the office.

ROSEMARY. I remember you saying it to me.

GERALD. I thought at the time that it was awfully unfair that he hadn't seen it for what it was, that he hadn't seen it as a likeness to himself. There he was, large as life, as unctuous as he appears in real life, the vile person that he is, being depicted in the most truthful way and failing to recognise the truth of it. I remember bursting into laughter when I saw him being represented on the screen.

ROSEMARY. I remember you laughing. And then you left the room. Still laughing. You'd come in for the secateurs.

GERALD. And he said he'd burst into laughter too.

ROSEMARY. How annoying. Did he say who he thought the toad was? The office toad.

GERALD. He just gave one of his toad-like grunts and scuttled away.

ROSEMARY. If it was an unpalatable truth about himself perhaps he didn't want to accept it. I don't see why he should.

GERALD. Why shouldn't he?

ROSEMARY. But it doesn't become an unpalatable truth unless you see something of yourself in it. In the portrayal.

GERALD. I saw it. Why shouldn't he?

ROSEMARY. But he did. But about someone else.

GERALD. It seems to me that people can delude themselves into the most far-fetched things about themselves. That some people are the authors of their own life stories, the most extraordinary fantasies about themselves. Wouldn't recognise an unpalatable truth about themselves if they saw one. Even when made perfectly clear to them. Ho, Ho, Ho, they go, and immediately the barriers go up and they think the representation they have seen refers to someone else. And not to them. It put me off my sorts for the rest of the day. Each day I now seem to be put off my sorts. Something happens. Something unexpected. Something inexplicable. Something unpalatable occurs . . .

ROSEMARY. But you surely don't think he was referring to you?

GERALD. What does it matter what I think? It only matters what they think. And how do I know what it is they are thinking? They may be thinking all sorts of things that are the opposite of the truth.

ROSEMARY. The truth as you see it.

GERALD. How else is one to see it?

ROSEMARY. They can't all be toads.

GERALD. They are all toads. Each and every one. He then went across to one of the other toads, whispered something into his ear, and then they both looked across at me and grinned. Now why did they do that?

ROSEMARY. But if you go around thinking that all the others are perfect toads why shouldn't all the others go around thinking that everyone else is a perfect toad?

GERALD. Why should I sit here and listen to unpalatable truths about others, which, I might add, might be perfectly palatable to me, if they don't see the truth in what has been said about themselves? If you are shown something unpalatable about yourself then you should be able to accept it.

ROSEMARY. I can't imagine anyone wanting to.

GERALD. I would be perfectly able to accept it.

ROSEMARY. I don't suppose you would.

GERALD. Do you ever get a glimpse of me?

ROSEMARY. Sometimes. Do you ever get a glimpse of me?

GERALD. Sometimes.

ROSEMARY. You never tell me.

GERALD. You never tell me.

ROSEMARY. I did that once. There's always something about the plays. Always something that upsets you.

GERALD. I never get in the least upset. It is all made up. Not a glimpse of the truth in it. It is the author scoring points. It is all water off a duck's back to me. Why do we watch the plays? He is probably in Majorca. Away from it all.

ROSEMARY. Who?

GERALD. The author. Probably sunning himself somewhere. Too disdainful even to watch the nonsense he has put together.

ROSEMARY. Well I like a play.

GERALD. I know you do.

ROSEMARY. You've never liked them.

GERALD. I am not interested in the author's point of view. What he has to say. His view of life. His view of things. Why should I be? I am not in the least interested in what he has to say. That he should even be allowed to say what he has to say in the first place. And then be paid for it!

ROSEMARY. That's because you're only interested in your own point of view.

GERALD. Has your own life ever been changed because of a play you've watched?

ROSEMARY. I don't think so.

GERALD. Has any play you've ever watched made you change the way you think?

ROSEMARY. I can't say it's changed the way I think. I don't think I'd want to change the way I think.

GERALD. You try putting across your own point of view and you watch the other fellow's face going blank. Can't wait until you've put across your point of view so that he can put his point of view back to you. Hasn't taken in a word of what you've said. And nowhere does anything he's saying relate back to what you've said. But the author? Nowhere to be seen when he's ramming his point of view down your throat. You can't answer back. You can talk to the set all night long for what good it'll do you.

ROSEMARY. Gerald. Loosen your collar. You've gone quite red.

GERALD. I am not getting hot under the collar if that's what you mean.

ROSEMARY. You're awfully worked up.

GERALD. I am not in the least worked up.

ROSEMARY. It's always the same when we watch a play together.

GERALD. But we are not watching the play.

ROSEMARY. I am.

GERALD. But how can you be watching the play when we are talking?

ROSEMARY. I can watch the play and talk.

GERALD. He should have seen himself in the representation of himself. That's all I am saying.

ROSEMARY. Who?

GERALD. The office toad.

ROSEMARY. But you said they were all toads.

GERALD. Then all of them. They should have all seen it. They should have all seen themselves in it. What is the point in having a representation of yourself if you cannot see yourself in it. That you somehow deflect it.

ROSEMARY. You've never seen a representation of yourself?

GERALD. No.

ROSEMARY. Not in that play within the play?

GERALD. I did not take it to be a representation of myself.

ROSEMARY. You didn't even see it.

GERALD. I did. I did see it.

ROSEMARY. You said you didn't.

GERALD. It doesn't matter what I said.

ROSEMARY. Then you do watch the plays. It reminded me of what you were. How you were. (*Pause*.) Gerald. Loosen your collar.

There is the sound of a police siren on the TV. It recedes.

It's about the collapse of law and order.

GERALD. What is?

ROSEMARY. The play.

GERALD. What play?

ROSEMARY. The play we are watching.

GERALD. But it doesn't look like a play to me at all.

ROSEMARY. What does it look like?

GERALD. It looks like a documentary.

ROSEMARY. But it's not a documentary. It's a play.

GERALD. But there can't be such squalor in the world. I refuse to
believe it. When it comes to the truth of the world I see about me I
prefer to believe that the evidence of what I see around me is the
truth of it all.

ROSEMARY. But it's not all that squalid. They haven't set fire to the
bed yet.

GERALD. They are asleep, but he hasn't put out his cigarette. There
was the sound of the police siren. Rioting in the streets very
probably. It is to do with squalor. It is to do with the collapse of
decent, civilised values.

ROSEMARY. It might be a love story. It might be about two people
falling in love against fearful odds. Anyway. It all looks very much
of a lull to me. Mother was right. I think I'll make some tea. Would
you like me to make you a cup?

GERALD. I think I'll have a brandy. A large one. I think I've earned it.

ROSEMARY. Must you drink so much?

GERALD. What else is there to do?

ROSEMARY (*concerned*). Gerald. Are you all right?

GERALD. Of course I'm all right. I've never felt better. I shall feel
better still when this nonsense is over.

ROSEMARY. I don't suppose much will happen now. Perhaps it's
one of those plays that starts off quite well and ends up as the most
fearful damp squib.

The TV is singing a Val Doonican song to itself.

ROSEMARY. Gerald.

A croak.

Oh, dear!

She switches channels and there is another play.
Music.

Gerald?

GERALD *collapses back into his chair.*

Gerald?

GERALD *groans.*

Gerald!

GERALD *gives a last gasp.*

Oh dear.

The telephone rings.

ROSEMARY. Mother! Yes. We were watching it too . . . I know. I
thought it was awfully poor. What I saw of it . . . You did too . . . ?
Mother. Gerald died . . . Just now. We'd just been watching the last
part of the play on the other side when I could see the most awful
lull coming up so I got up and made a cup of tea and when I came
back into the room the play had ended and there was this most
awful music programme on so I changed the side and there was this
other play on and Gerald was standing with his back to the set with
a look of complete disbelief on his face. He was pointing to the set,
it was almost as though he was about to say something and then he
gave a croak. Then he collapsed back into the chair. Then he gave
his last gasp. Well I think it was his last gasp. It sounded very much
like a last gasp. Mother. I've got to call the doctor. Mother. You saw
the play. Was anything said? In the play? Something that might have
touched Gerald on a raw nerve . . . ? They were squatters? Well he
hated squatters . . . And Marxists too. Well he hated Marxists . . .
But, Mother, what a cruel thing to say. He wasn't in the least bit
faceless. He hated scruffs. He didn't like the indolent. He hated the
work-shy. But he'd go out of his way to help anyone genuinely in
need. As long as they knew their proper station in life. He'd bend
over backwards . . . No. I never knew what he really thought about
things. He never said much. He was very secretive . . . No. But the
plays had given him quite a few slaps in the face over the years.
Quite a few shocks. Of course, he never took any notice.

The sound of an ambulance siren from the TV.

Oh, dear.

(*Back on the phone*): Mother. Are you still there . . . ? It was all
water off a duck's back, according to Gerald. He never took a bit of
notice . . . You didn't see the end either . . . ? And then there was
that frightful singer. So I suppose we'll never know what was said.
Something must have upset him. It seemed too poor a piece for
them to show it again. So I suppose we'll never know . . . Mother.
I must call the doctor . . . Yes. I'll see you on Sunday . . . Yes.
We'll still be able to go for a drive.

She puts down the phone.

Gerald?

She picks up the phone and dials a number.

Doctor. It's Rosemary Harrison. Lauderdale Road. I know it's late.

It's my husband. I think he died. Just now . . . Of course I'm not sure. I just think he has . . . You'll come quickly? . . . Thank you.

She puts the phone down.

Gerald?

Silence.

Television audible.

WOMAN. Oh, dear. He's gone quite grey.

DOCTOR. He's bound to. It's very possible that he's dead.

The sound of an ambulance from the TV. The sound of a real ambulance.
Both cut out.

The end.

The following is the text of the TV play which plays behind the main text.

DOCTOR. We ought to get him to the hospital.

WOMAN. Good of you to come so quickly. He was sitting there just as usual and then suddenly seemed to go 'snap'. But he often made snapping sounds when he was watching television.

DOCTOR. Very faint pulse. Hardly discernible. May I use the phone?

WOMAN. Of course.

DOCTOR. What sort of a life did he lead?

WOMAN. Oike most other people. Unremarkable. Hated what was going on around him. But who doesn't? Thought the world was going to pot. Quite right. Thought all the decent values. All gone.

DOCTOR. We live in a changing world.

WOMAN. He was always saying that.

DOCTOR. No exercise?

WOMAN. Not if he could help it.

DOCTOR. Did he eat a lot?

WOMAN. Never stopped.

DOCTOR. Drink a lot?

WOMAN. He loved a drink.

DOCTOR (*on the phone*). Charing Cross? . . . Doctor Finsbury. I want an ambulance. 17, Wilton Avenue. Cardiac arrest. Thank you. (*Phone down.*) They'll be here soon.

WOMAN. I sometimes think he thought life had become awfully unfair. He was always saying how unfair he thought life was. Decay. Everywhere. He was always talking about that.

DOCTOR. You say he snapped. You heard it?

WOMAN. It was like the sound of a piece of elastic going.

DOCTOR. I'll attempt to get his heart going again.

WOMAN. Oh, do try.

DOCTOR (*grunts*). Carrying a lot of weight.

WOMAN. Wouldn't walk a step. Not if he could help it. Thought it was all propaganda.

DOCTOR (*grunt*). What was?

WOMAN. Everything. No one knowing their proper place any more. Things like that. Everything in the hands of the wrong sort of people, things like that.

DOCTOR (*grunt*). Everything was conspiring against him?

WOMAN. Yes.

DOCTOR (*grunt*). I sometimes feel like that. (*Grunt.*) Medicine is not what it was. (*Grunt.*) Pill pusher! (*Grunt.*) Sickness notes to the idle and disaffected. (*Grunt.*) No backbone to the nation. (*Grunt.*) Instead of prolonging life! (*Grunt.*) I should be trying to shorten it.

WOMAN. My husband had plenty of backbone.

DOCTOR (*grunt*). Just pushing the pills.

WOMAN. He's gone quite grey.

DOCTOR (*grunt*). He's bound to. It's very possible that he's dead.

THE OLD MAN SLEEPS ALONE

A legend, for radio,
of the building of Durham Cathedral

by John Arden

John Arden was born in Yorkshire in 1930. His plays include *Live Like Pigs* (1958) and *Serjeant Musgrave's Dance* (1959) staged at the Royal Court Theatre; *The Workhouse Donkey* (Chichester Festival 1963), *Armstrong's Last Goodnight* (Glasgow Citizens' Theatre 1964; National Theatre) and *Left-Handed Liberty* (Mermaid Theatre 1965). His plays written in collaboration with Margaretta D'Arcy include *The Business of Good Government* (1960), *The Happy Haven* (1960), *Ars Longa, Vita Brevis* (1963), *Friday's Hiding* (1965), *The Royal Pardon* (1966), *The Hero Rises Up* (1968), *The Ballygombeen Bequest* (1972), *The Island of the Mighty* (1972), *Keep the People Moving* (for radio 1972), *The Non-Stop Connolly Show* (Liberty Hall, Dublin, 1975) and *Vandleur's Folly* (7:84 Theatre Company, 1978). His radio play *Pearl* received a special Giles Cooper Award in 1978, and he has also written for television. In 1982 his first novel, *Silence Among the Weapons* was short-listed for the Booker McConnell Prize for Fiction.

The Old Man Sleeps Alone was first broadcast on BBC Radio 4 on 22nd October 1982. The cast was as follows:

SAINT CUTHBERT ⎫
BISHOP'S CLERK ⎬   Ronald Baddiley

NICK SQUINCH, *a young stone-mason*   Nigel Anthony
THE FRENCHMAN, *master-mason*   Geoffrey Banks
CHARLIE BONES, *a young stone-mason*   Christian Rodska
THE FRENCHMAN'S DAUGHTER   Linda Gardner
ALICE, *a paramour*   Lesley Nicol
PRIOR'S CLERK   Malcolm Hebden
THE BISHOP   Frank Middlemass
THE PRIOR   David Calder
A YOUNG PRENTICE   Kevin Kennedy

CURATE ⎫
JACK, *a journeyman* ⎬   Russell Dixon

Director Alfred Bradley

Notes on the main characters

NICK and CHARLIE are both in their middle twenties: they need clear differentiation of voices. NICK is bluff, blustering, extrovert. CHARLIE lacks self-confidence, except within his own imagination. When his imagination is let loose, it soars.

THE FRENCHMAN is about fifty; he is filled to his last breath with enormous pride in himself and his work, which carries with it a peculiar contemptuous malice toward all others.

The FRENCHMAN'S DAUGHTER combines in herself the pride and the self-sufficiency of her father. But this is distorted by the extreme difficulty of her position as a female with an unwontedly specialised education — her relations with the men of her father's craft inevitably take on aspects of venality and blackmail, which in turn fills her with self-contempt.

The two CLERKS are officious mouthpieces for their masters. The PRIOR'S CLERK has also a certain knowledge of his intellectual superiority — or rather, of his keener practicality — in contrast to the PRIOR. ALICE is a good-natured and affectionate young woman, superficially censorious and caustic.

The PRIOR is an intolerant authoritarian, an obscurant.

The BISHOP is a man of enormous secular as well as ecclesiastical responsibilities, effectively the viceroy of the whole of the north of England. His ability to fulfil his role is not diminished by his apparent aesthetic frivolity. He despises the PRIOR.

General Note

There was in fact a transference of the late-12th-century chapel from
the east end to the west at Durham. And St Cuthbert was traditionally
held responsible for this. My own interpretation of the story was
suggested by the observable strong contrast between the Romanesque
styles of the chapel and the rest of the cathedral. The designer of the
chapel — one feels — would have built in pointed Gothic, had he been
in closer touch with the centres of this new taste, further south. As it
was, he produced a rather odd piece of work, clumsy and elegant at
one and the same time, archaic and innovatory. For the purposes of
the story I have made the inaccurate assumption that the main
structure of the cathedral was completed only just before the chapel
was commenced. In fact it is known to have been built at the end of
the previous century, and its designer cannot have survived into the
reign of Henry II. (Also, it was not, in fact, the first stone church on
the site.)

A note on the speech patterns of the various characters.
NICK and CHARLIE are supposed to be indigenous English, as is also
the CURATE, and — with allowance for his superior breeding — the
PRIOR: whereas the two CLERKS and the BISHOP are Normans.
A non-specific 'Northumbrian' quality should therefore be apparent
in the voices of the English — less a 'regional accent' than a broadening
of vowels and a hardening of consonants. The Normans speak more
thinly — as it were. The FRENCHMAN and his DAUGHTER can have a
slight foreign intonation, just sufficient to remind the listener that they
are from foreign parts, originally.

Scene One

The sound of wind and sea, waves against rocks, gulls. Out of this grows the voice of CUTHBERT, *singing the Anglican hymn 'Holy Holy Holy Lord God Almighty.' The words of the hymn are now loud, now faint and covered by the sea-noises. He reaches 'Casting down their golden crowns around the glassy sea!' on a crescendo: and then breaks off. The sea-noises fade down as he speaks: a sombre grumbling flat toneless voice as of a man several hundred years dead and lost somewhere among the vastness of nature.*

CUTHBERT. In those days, long ago, oh Redeemer so long long time ago, because I, Cuthbert, brought the strength of Christ to this fierce people, because I died upon the very edge of this fierce people, upon an island, within the fringe of the grey sea, north-easterly, cold: there came thieves and murderers, in their ships, out of the north, over the sea. And those among whom I was buried had no choice but to dig me up and carry me with them to whatever safety they could find. A word came to them saying, 'Follow the cow'. They found a brown cow feeding . . .

The sound of a cow grazing, mooing occasionally, and shuffling footfalls on a grassy path.

With the box of my bones on their shoulders they followed her, until the day that she stopped still. They put down the box, took spades and made a hole in the ground, covered the earth over, buried me.

The sound of earth thudding on a coffin lid.

It was on top of a rock beside a rough river, you could see far across through moor and mountain from that place. They made a dwelling for themselves, like a cloister, out of wood and clay. And they bode there and worshipped. What happened to the cow? She was a sign, she served her purpose, she took herself off. What more d'you want to know about her? The years went past, the fashions of men changed, wood and clay began to be scorned. My box was still of wood. And I lived in it, dead.

Fade out sound effects.

Scene Two

NICK (*as narrator*).
    A better man than the Frenchman
    Never built with stone,
    The most cunning master-mason
    Northumbria had ever seen,
    Made arch and vault of this great minster:
    And now he's dead and gone.

    Nave built, choir built, house of the shave-head monks, all built in
well-carved freestone: our second Henry, Plantagenet, being
undisputed king, very little warfare left in the land, plenty of
taxation gold for good structure. He said, afore he died, the
Frenchman: 'as far as *I'm* done,' he said, 'it's finished, *finie. c'est
complète, la belle église*. What else is to be rendered for it,' he said,
'up to you, my two bold prentices, English, the lads I taught. If
there's work yet to be done on the church, you do it. Ah, but
which one of you will be master? There's a question.' There we
stood, the pair of us, either side of his bed's head. I looked
across at the other one — Charlie Bones, crooked Charlie, black
angel with the visage of death, aye a death's head at a death bed
and don't think I didn't take note of it. Jacob and Esau, we stood
there, in receipt of the old tyrant's blessing. All those years he had
kept us down, now — it seemed — he gave us our life. It's an odd
thing how he passed out of his own. An acclaimed master-mason,
done his work all over the world, Normandy, Picardy, Flanders, and
now Northumbria, to stumble like a daft lad on a badly-braced
scaffold-gantry eighteen feet above the pavement, could that be
called expected? I could have shifted the ties of that scaffold myself,
had I thought on it, I felt that mad towards his foul temper: but I
didn't. Did anyone? Refer it to Charlie. I make no accusation.
Mind you, neither did the Frenchman. Put out one hand, caught
hold of mine: with fading breath he talked in English. 'Charlie,' he
said —

FRENCHMAN (*speaking with difficulty*). Charlot —

CHARLIE (*as narrator*). Nick, he said —

FRENCHMAN. Nicholas — when the Prince-Bishop compelled me here
    from my own country and commanded me build, in such a
    wilderness, what was there to be seen upon this naked rock and stone?
    The rude tomb of a dead saint, your Cuthbert long long time dead,
    an old savage holy man: and some inferior small cabins, wood and
    clay, barbaric crudity . . . And I did build. I chose my workmen out
    of all the north parts of England, you, my two young men, start-to-
    finish I instructed you not-quite-every secret of my occult and
    marvellous craft. I instructed you in anger, rage and impatience: you
    were brutish, you did not love me. Why should you? I did not love
    you: only the work. And were you or were you not good for it? So

now then: who is the best to continue to command it? It is a
question. Ah, the question of the strength of your mind. Which
one of you, which . . . ?

CHARLIE (*as narrator*). Oh, but there was no doubt, I was the best, me.
Charlie and nowt but Charlie to carry the crown of the craft for
ever. So why would he never give it me? All I got was the slap of his
hand, filthy French words — never mind gaping up at the soaring
of your arch-tops, he'd say: your job's to cut that window-sill one
handspan back to the chamfer, and you've not *done* it, damn your
eyes, aye, in French. Whereas the other one, Nick Squinch — *he*
never laid a stone wrong in his whole service. And yet to what
purpose? For he never laid a stone *right,* neither, except to another
man's do-this-here do-that-there continuous wet-nurse direction . . .
Though someone did lay the bracing of a scaffold-pole wrong, I
know that. I make no accusation. If I'd not been so slow and
stupid, I'd have done it myself three months ago. Could carve
myself into a gargoyle I so failed my opportunity: three months ago
was the one time I ever got one French word of comfort. For the
conception of a statue-niche on either side of the refectory porch
when Nick Squinch would have left it three beast-like feet of blind
wall. Why didn't I do it then and hooked in with my claim in the
height of favour? As always, too slow. But no accusation: refer it
to Nick, that's all . . .

NICK (*as narrator*). So there he lay, silent, French breath, indefatigable,
kept on coming . . . how long to die?

The FRENCHMAN *wheezes and gasps. The* CURATE *can be heard,
pattering the Latin words of the last rites.*

(*As narrator*). The needful priest with his bottle of oil, the required
prayers for his safe transporting —

CURATE. *In manus tuas, Domine . . .*

NICK (*as narrator*). Three men around one man and at his feet to make
it five, one more immortal soul, hers.

CHARLIE (*as narrator*). She knelt at the bed's end, staring right into
her father's eyes, you could have cut her out of crystal.

NICK (*as narrator*). Red hair, red freckles upon skin like sour cheese,
short-fingered hands pressed together in front of what claimed to
be an unfingered bosom: her round red mouth a tight closed fist in
a glove of soft silk.

CHARLIE (*as narrator*). To Nick Squinch and me he had bequeathed
the skill of his trade, the tools of his trade, equal between us, he said
so. He had one more bequest.

NICK (*as narrator*). Into the ear of the curate. We couldn't hear a word
of it. The curate told.

There is whispering from the FRENCHMAN. *The* CURATE *repeats aloud what he says.*

CURATE. Sirs: he says, this young woman, his one child from his dead French wife. He says, either or both of you would be wed to her, if you could, he has observed it. But where *her* mind in the matter should be, there is, he says, a question —

NICK. Aye aye then, come on with it, tell us —

CHARLIE. How can he tell us if you talk over the top of him, will you let the man speak!

CURATE. He says: to his daughter alone he has contrived to teach the one secret of his craft he has not passed on to you. Protection, he says, for the sole mastery of the trade. Protection. I think he's laughing.

NICK. Grace of God, is that all!

The whispers begin again.

CURATE. Ssh — ssh — he's still talking. Sirs, wait, don't crowd over. He says: to whom she chooses to bring the skill that he has given her, to that man she shall be wife: and he shall be master of the work. He says: I, his last confessor, I am to be witness, and convey his word to the Prince-Bishop that the great church may be completed and so fulfil the Bishop's dream of Christianity, Sovereignty, the Beauty of Holiness in the waste places of this uncouth kingdom. He says that. He says now he will sing a little song, in our English, for his last goodnight.

FRENCHMAN (*singing, in a careful but feeble voice*).
'A better man than the Frenchman
Never built with stone.
Who can say how he should come
So strangely tumbling down?'

NICK. Eh, what's this . . . ?

CHARLIE. Aye, what is it?

(*Speaking as narrator*). Half-blind eyes of the dying man all of a sudden as bright as quicksilver —

NICK (*as narrator*). But who are they looking at? Him? Me? Last-minute accusation should be dead accurate or not at all.

CHARLIE. The least he could have given us was the strength to point a finger . . .

FRENCHMAN (*uttering phrases at random*). *I* don't know . . . they don't know . . . she don't know . . . he don't know. Which one. Let them, to themselves, enquire. About which one. I have, to them all, left behind me sufficient contention. Let them contend, who is the best. Let them enquire, who was the worst.

CHARLIE (*as narrator*). So he died.

NICK (*as narrator*). And there we were.

CURATE. If he had to meddle at the end with rhyme and music, a Psalm of David would have done better to have got him to God. Very like he didn't know any. T't t't . . . French of course.

DAUGHTER (*as narrator*). So there we were. And all the choice, the decision, the deed of contention, is now mine.

Scene Three

DAUGHTER (*as narrator*). It never occurred to me I should not make choice of one of them — they were both now made free of their apprentice-indenture, both now admitted to Mastery in the guild. If I am not to be wed to the new master of the minster work, I must become either a nun or a harlot, I suppose. But I had not been expecting it would be me who would *make* the new master. For whatever contorted reason in the cruel brain of my father. So cruel he had been to me indeed. So blessed the loosened pole that let down the scaffold-plank under the dint of his proud foot.

The sounds of singing — a requiem in an echoing church.

DAUGHTER (*as narrator*). Behind a pillar of the transept, during an interval of the solemn obsequy, I drew Nick a little apart from the train of mourners. He being the one whom my body had desired for many months, his golden hair, his long strong neck — neck of an archangel perched with a trumpet among columns of the clerestory over the altar of Christ. My body said, 'choose Nick.'

NICK (*in a hoarse eager whisper*). Me? You have chosen *me*?

DAUGHTER (*business-like*). I know very well that you know how to lay stone in precise order, how to carve mouldings as clear and straight as the banner-staves of a marching army. I do *not* know that you know how to make use of the gift that has been entrusted to me.

NICK (*impatient*). What is all this? What *is* this marvellous gift?

DAUGHTER. Ssh: they say prayers over my father. Hard enough for him to get where he should go, without your interrupting it. Nick, are we good friends?

NICK. In as little as I've ever been allowed to talk to you, yes.

DAUGHTER. Then after this we stay close friends, whenever you like: from now on I make certain I am held in no prison. Do you know what I am telling you? Dear Nick, do you not know?

NICK (*as narrator*). One warm damp hand pressed into my hand, under the fold of my cloak, oh aye, it did tell me. Told me moreover that she was not to be my wife . . .

(*Speaking to her*). Greed of God, girl, you've chosen *him!*

DAUGHTER. For my father's gift, yes. For *my* gift, I have chosen *you*.

NICK. Be damned if I'm dealing with this for a game. There's more to be said, much more . . . !

The sound of chanting increases as though a procession is moving out of the church.
Fade out.

Scene Four

DAUGHTER (*as narrator*). I had hoped he would have been: philosophical: regretful of course: but, resignation. Ah no, too much to hope. These northern boys make anger the only indulgence of their heart. We shall see. My brain had said, Charlie Bones: but I could never find good reason why brain and body could not alike be both satisfied. I came home after the funeral to my father's empty house-place: I sent an old woman for Charlie.

CHARLIE (*as narrator*). Oh I'd seen the pair of 'em, both at it, in the church, two heads of hair, sand-red and sunstroke-gold, wrapped up like it seemed in the one black muffling mantle, squashed faces, hands clenched under drape of the cloth. It's a wonder I bothered to go when she called for me.

The sound of a knock on a door, the door opens, the sound of feet entering the house. He speaks to her.

CHARLIE. Hello there then, French daughter: so despite all you sent for me. All right then, where's Nick? I'd thought he'd have been with you already, making holiday for his pride of place.

DAUGHTER. He's not here, he went straight down-river, a boat-load of Normandy limestone, to be brought up for the work, he said.

CHARLIE. That stone won't be needed till next month, he's gone for it already?

(*To himself*). All signed and settled then, she's given him the full word, by God: or he shows his confidence!

DAUGHTER (*insinuating*). But when the stone comes here, who is it will determine how and where the cargo will be laid . . . ?

CHARLIE (*catching her tone: but very suspicious*). Eh . . . ? Are you telling me then that *he* won't?

DAUGHTER *laughs, slightly.*

CHARLIE (*angry*). You're making mock, you shifty bitch; I'll not
believe it, never. Let me tell you summat of truth between me and
Nick Squinch — very grand, he can carve mouldings, lay stone, his
finished course-work neat as silk from the weaving of a fine loom.
But between him and me there's only one of us knows how to frame
in the mind foundations, pavement, walls, piers, pillars and roof,
and all to be included in a complete, topped, comely structure that'd
turn folk's heads for ever to gaze at it and talk. And that one is not
Nick. And that one is the only one should ever dare claim the name
of Master. (*Pause.*) So now then. All right, you've chosen. When
golden geese are all in favour, dirty ducks keep their own end of the
pond. I knew what the Frenchman thought of me, it's little wonder
you'd think the same.

(*Speaking as narrator*). She said nowt for a long time, except —

DAUGHTER. Charlie: sit down, please. Do not be so foolish.

CHARLIE (*as narrator*). I had meant to storm out on her: but
somehow it didn't seem the right shape for this meeting. So I sat. On
a lump of sheepskin. Her father's hearth-stone, under cramped and
sooty beams, half-built pinnacles of the minster like giants' teeth
above our heads, half-built work that could be mine, had ought to
be mine . . . nay, it *was* mine: because she now told me. Told me
this same minute with a hot hand creeping in where no-one to my
best belief but yellow-haired Nick Squinch had ever felt it creep
before.

DAUGHTER. You are an ugly little black creature —

CHARLIE (*as narrator*). — she said.

DAUGHTER. Black, twisted, yet lives inside you great churches and
houses of glory, so many mansions for the huge Jerusalem, spired
and roofed with gold, such as my father — whatever else he did —
had as his dream night after night: it was his true dream, I assure
you of that; just as here, now, today, I am assured it is yours also.
But never Nick's. No not his: so I choose you and for no mockery.

CHARLIE (*as narrator*). She was right, of course, though how could
she have known it? Only unless that bloody Frenchman had told
her.

(*Speaking to her*). If he told you, why didn't he tell me?

DAUGHTER. It was never his taste to give praise to those in need of
it. To me, for example, never: though I deserved it more than many.

CHARLIE. How?

DAUGHTER. Oh in good time you'll find out. Or why else are you
here?

CHARLIE. He gave praise enough to Nick Squinch.

DAUGHTER. Only to bring you down: whenever he spoke well to Nick, what was it for? For uncovering some fault you had made in your haste, was it not?

CHARLIE. A man can't be right all the time.

DAUGHTER. A man can try. Must try: Or the greatest work of all his thought will fall to pieces like rotten bogwood.

CHARLIE. Dammit, woman, I know that: don't talk out of the gob of your dead father to me.

DAUGHTER. Why else are you here? My father knew what was wrong with you. But he was a jealous cruel man, his jealousy did not allow him to ever tell you where you did right. Now Charlie, *I* have told you, so do not you say to me I am the same as him. For I hated him and I thank the Mother of God that he is dead. Filthy French words, hard slaps of his hand, or his belt, or his brassbound three-foot measuring-rod were all I ever got for the day-in day-out hard usage of my brain he put me to all these years, so that he and he alone could take benefit. Today it is my turn to let *you* to take that benefit, my turn, my own choice. Prove yourself worthy. And do not despise Nick. You will require such as him for a permanent correction: for the faults you will make in your haste . . . Now —

CHARLIE (*as narrator*). I had thought for a few moments the deeds of Venus were in prospect on this hearth-stone: but no, it seemed that that had been only a way, like, to broach open her chief business. The inner mystery of her father's trade, you see, wherewith she alone had been confided . . .

DAUGHTER. I am talking of what you can find even today practised in parts of France, and beyond in Italy, where some of the craft can still remember what was done by the masters of Rome, ancient days, when the world was wise. My father in a fashion had it, but not complete. To make complete he would have had to be able to read and write and to accomplish numbers, divide and multiply according to the science of the Arabians — he could never learn this.

CHARLIE. Arabians — you mean heathen magic?

DAUGHTER. If you will . . . And it can be taught. Ssh. He made me learn it, so I could work it for him. He found a Jew in the city of York, condemned to the traffic of usury for his infidel religion: but this man was very curious in his knowledge of these hidden arts. Month after month he made me visits in deep secret till I was filled to the top of my skull with all that my father required. And thereby, when my father conceived the pride and primacy of some great new structure, it was possible for myself to shape all of it upon parchment for him before ever one stone was laid, or one trench dug, or even a yard of ground squared out with string. You will have seen some of these parchments — ?

CHARLIE. Never parchments, no. Drafts, we called drafts, that he
lined out with charcoal on whitewashed boards, and that — but —

DAUGHTER. They were marked upon parchment first; and far more
marked on the parchment than ever he'd copy upon boards for
you and the workmen to see. Sssh, sh, look at these . . .

CHARLIE (*as narrator*). She lit a candle, held it low, shovelled the fire
to one side, and lifted the hearth-stone: slow, careful, pricking
up her ears for fear.

An appropriate sound effect.

Oh and there she had it: hidden beneath the heat:
Flat box filled to the brim with flowing lines and figures,
Deployed draft of every detail her father could devise,
Measurings, mode and module, meticulous proportion
Of an entire sacred city begotten in the spirit of one man
And recorded for the rightful reward of whoever could next
    regulate it best —
Me: she was making it mine: the majesty of my work
To be fabricate in the future and made firm for all time
Through just such pen-and-ink, precise calculus, oh permanence
    of proven power!

(*Speaking to her*). Why, with this I can shape buildings as though
Lucifer laid stone for me by night!

DAUGHTER. Aha, you do see it! I knew you would be able to see it.
I'll just say one thing: Nick will despise this, but we do not despise
him. The ease of his careful handcraft is *needed*, Charlie —

CHARLIE. Not on any job of mine, begod: don't like him, don't
need him, won't have him —

DAUGHTER. If not him, then someone else of the same nature, I
am warning. Unless you yourself can make yourself of that nature . . .
Can you?

CHARLIE (*as narrator*). Before it grew morning, she did try some
passage toward a few of the deeds of Venus: the first survey of an
un-pegged-out site, I took it for. I was also able to take it, she was
none too pleased with the state of the ground. Aye well, perhaps
not important. She *had* said I was black and ugly . . . Truth . . .

Scene Five

*Fade in the sound of wind, and the noises of a barge being brought into
a quay — splashes, shoutings, the trample of a horse, etc.*

NICK (*as narrator*). It's a coarse business in a cross-wind, to bring a
deep-laden barge to the wharf below the minster — cursing and
roaring and hauling on wet ropes, always one silly bugger gets into

the water over the top of his boots, that morning it were me —

He plunges into the water and curses, among shouts from the workmen.

NICK. Damnation to bloody hellfire . . . !

JACK. Are you right, Nick?

NICK. Get me out of it, sharp!

More splashings and cursings.

NICK. And what the devil d'you reckon you're on, Jack Rabbet, fart-arsing around down here at the riverside when I'd told you to be up the north-west tower putting pointwork on the joints of that corbel-table?

(*He shouts to the others*). Watch out with them slings for godsake, you'll have half of your load in the stream!

(*To* JACK *again*). Jack, I asked you a question. Well?

JACK. Charlie Bones said to give over the corbel-table while further orders.

NICK. Oh, so he's calling himself master already, is he? I daresay the Prior and Chapter'll have an opinion about that.

(*Speaking as narrator*). For as soon as the Frenchman died, Charlie and me made a sort of bond: neither one of us'd take over anything until regular agreement with the great churchmen in charge, which needed both of us present and willing. Pending which, we'd each hold on to the portions of work we'd already in hand.

(*Speaks to* JACK). Pending which, my portion of work, Jack, was the upper stages of the north-west tower.

JACK. Nay, the work on the tower's altogether given over —

PRIOR'S CLERK (*approaching*). Master Nicholas, may we have a word?

NICK (*outraged*). Given over? All of it? Greed of God, what's been going on — !

JACK. Now, Nick, don't blame me —

PRIOR'S CLERK (*repeats*). Master Nicholas . . .

JACK. The Father Prior's sent his clerk down to have a word and make it formal . . .

PRIOR'S CLERK. You see, his Grace the Lord Bishop has determined, with some abruptness (it is his prerogative), to cease all present work upon the edifice and immediately divert every major resource, both diocesan and monastic revenue, to the design and construction of a new chapel at the east end, to be dedicated to Our Blessed Lady. Our Lady, being a woman, he says, must be gratified upon the spontaneous instant.

NICK. That's all very well, but —

PRIOR'S CLERK. But of course, you will readily see, that the appointment of a master-mason for the new work had therefore to be made in immediate haste. According to the chaplain who attended the last hours of the late master from France (whom we all —

NICK. I know all about his last hours, I was there; and there's more to be said about —

PRIOR'S CLERK. — (whom we all most sincerely lament), this appointment should be afforded to his son-in-law, Master Charles.

NICK. Son-in-law? Already? Why it's not been a week yet —

PRIOR'S CLERK. It is true the nuptial was celebrated in haste. But the Prior does believe, sir, that the Lord Bishop's urgency makes it imperative to grant this contract to a craftsman with appreciable experience of this very particular site, and of its workmen, with all their concomitant contrarieties. Most unwise to search abroad for some stranger, however notable within the guild. After all, if the deceased master did not know the qualifications of his pupils, who should?

NICK (*as narrator*). I set no stiff neck against living as another man's deputy. Unless of course, the other man should by happenstance be Charlie Bones . . . It seemed though, that Charlie's wife had not thought about this 'unless'. Oh she had been looking forward to Nick Squinch as a convenient deputy. She met me that very same morning, on the path leading up from the wharf, had been waiting there, no doubt, while the Prior's clerk concluded his nonsense.

Fade out.

Scene Six

Fade in the sound of wind, as before. NICK's footfall on a stone path. The shouts and other noises of the barge-unloading are now distant, but continue.

DAUGHTER. Nick.

The sound of his footfalls stop.

DAUGHTER. Dear Nick, you have not yet unloaded your stone.

NICK. Charlie's stone now, for the Blessed Virgin, no less. Let him sort it, I'm finished.

DAUGHTER. No! He will need you. Nick, I beg you, do not go! You are needed here, Nick, on the work, Charlie Bones needs all your quality — and Nick —

NICK. Charlie Bones needs bloody nowt o'me but an iron toecap up the cleft of his rump: if I bide here much longer he'll get it, for all I'm a peace-seeking man.

DAUGHTER. Nick, not only Charlie — *I* need you, Nick. You did say, you know, there was so much more to say — why cannot you stay here, let us find the time to say it . . . ?

NICK. Aye, I suppose while Charlie walks all night on his scaffold-gantry, planning out the next botch for his job. Because from now on, I can tell you, the future of this contract'll be midnight dreams of glory and half-cock daytime botching, and that's all it'll be! I'm not stopping to witness it, let alone have any part of it! Which makes me mad because I thought once I could have — would have . . . coped, love, like a fit husband, for a woman of your sort: I did, I did truly . . . No: I won't bide.

The sound of his footsteps, going briskly away.

DAUGHTER (*calling after him*). But — but — oh Nick, where will you go — ?

NICK (*stopping a few yards away*). Newcastle . . . York . . . Fountains Abbey? Who knows? I want straight work and no nonsense: and I'll find it. Good-bye.

He starts walking away again. She begins to run after him.

DAUGHTER. I can't bear to live all my life with him and without you! Nick — if only you'd come back, I — I could loosen the scaffold-pole, and he'd fall like my father — !

His footsteps stop.

NICK (*in an appalled voice*). You said what? You said *what*!

DAUGHTER (*angry at herself for going too far*). Oh nothing, you heard what I said, it meant nothing.

NICK (*after a long time*). Greed of God, after that: after that, for the sake of all three of us, I'm on the road with no more words.

The sound of his feet going away again fast.
She bursts into angry tears.

DAUGHTER (*raging*). Go on then go go go go go-o-o — you yellow curdled *merde*, don't think I haven't seen her in your house-place, grinning at you, waiting there at fall of sunset for the brawn of bastard back . . . !

(*Speaking as narrator*). He didn't even give me thanks I was so discreet as never to have mentioned before his present concubine, or whatever she is. And I would not have been jealous of her, the stupid fat housewife thing: he could have had both of us and been happy, been so happy here. Or so I said, to myself, over and over, that dreary night and the next night, in the twisting bed of Charlie Bones — for he never was one to lie straight out and quiet when he slept, like a crab between my blankets, bony, biting, click click click, horrible shell and pincers, ugh. And then, on the third day, I saw Nick Squinch's young woman, laughing as loud as a cuckoo with a blood-smothered butcher-boy of a soldier at the top of the market. He had left her behind and had taken his road alone . . . He had left her, she meant nothing to him. What could this be, but a token that *I* meant so *much* to him that he could not bear to live within my reach . . . ?

Fade out.

Scene Seven

NICK (*as narrator*). I went straightway away from her, I went down to bid goodbye to the one I'd been keeping — Alice her name was: I did ask would she come with me, she said, no, tramping roads was no balm of Egypt for the soles of *her* feet: but both arms went round my neck, warmth, tenderness, a tear or two even, I don't forget it. Straightway I set boot on the road. York, by considered thought — another big minster building at York, and new churches rose up there at every street-corner; oh, I'd find work in York, very like master's work, if I set my hopes modest enough. Aye, and in due course I did find it. Reconstruction of a barbican gate for the captain of the castle. Modest. I kept on with it all that year.

Scene Eight

Fade in the sound of a bed creaking and a confused grunting.

DAUGHTER (*half asleep and irritable*). Crab. Ugly crab. Cut your toenails, why don't you?

CHARLIE *grunts and groans and tosses about.*

DAUGHTER. Oh God what are you doing, man: can you not sleep?

CHARLIE. No I can't sleep. It's too thick, far too clumsy, like a —

DAUGHTER. What's too thick?

CHARLIE. God it's like a great slab of cold-frozen porridge, I can't rid myself of — of —

DAUGHTER. Oh wake up and speak in order. What *is* it, is far too thick?

CHARLIE (*more coherently*). I can't rid myself of your damned old dad, his columns and arches in nave and choir. I'll tell you what's too thick: the whole notion of this chapel. It's for a lady, delicate lady, right, Mother of God to whom you talk so much, don't you, when you think I'm not listening.

DAUGHTER. She will protect me from the consequence, She only She —

CHARLIE. What consequence? Never mind now, I'm thinking about this chapel. He built the church for what he called the old savage holy man, Cuthbert, the buried saint: strong, solid, right. But not for Her. Delicate, slender, stretch out the hard stone till it takes on the shape of ivory: where's a candle, let's look at those parchments?

DAUGHTER. Dark midnight and the fire's gone out. Leave it till the morning.

CHARLIE. No no, I can't wait, we've got to remake all these drafts. Nine columns to hold the roof up, that's on the contract. Suppose we make it twelve, three rows of four instead of three to each row, if we do that we could cut down the dimension of each one by — by maybe as much as a half? I want all this redrafted, I've to transfer it to my working-boards by Tuesday, I promised the foreman they'd have all work and quantities for each gang disposed by Tuesday — get your ink out, your pen, it'll take you hours to redraft all this lot.

Fade music up and down to suggest the passage of time.

Scene Nine

A rustle of parchments.

CHARLIE. There we are, that's it, for a start, for a start at least — I don't like the shape of that blank wall — bring in more arches and of course we've lowered the height of them.

DAUGHTER. It is a very heavy wall on the top of your slim columns.

CHARLIE. Patterns carved round all the arches, paintwork, white and blue: take all the weight away, carry it away, light as the sky.

DAUGHTER. I'm not talking of the proportions, as they appear to the eyesight. I have given you the rules of the mathematic for them, I *know* they are exact. I am asking you rather, is the weight of the stone safe upon such slim columns? This is masoncraft, not mathematic: I do not know the answer.

CHARLIE. *I* do. Of course it's safe. Is the chapel beautiful or isn't it?

DAUGHTER. It will be beautiful beyond words: but —

CHARLIE. Then that's it then. Good God, it's broad morning and no

fire lit. What the devil do we have for breakfast? Nowt, I suppose,
as usual.

Scene Ten

NICK (*as narrator*). It was well past Yuletide I heard word from the
north, word about Charlie Bones. Now mind, I didn't seek to hear
owt about him, not at all, vacant void, me, of all curiosity. But
there, by the daftest chance, it was this girl, Alice, you'll bear in
mind — all of a sudden there she stands, one hand on her round
hip, in the soldiers' garth of York Castle, with a bucket to be
filled at the well. Eh, dear, had she come down to chase me?

The sounds of bustle and talk among soldiers' wives etc. at the well.

ALICE. Lay claim on Nick Squinch's good nature? Whatever next?
Eh, Love-of-Christ, but it's good to see you, Nick.

NICK (*as narrator*). After I'd left her, she'd taken up with a tall soldier.
Six battles beyond the border in Scotland he'd felt not a blood-
scratch of hurt: but as he and old greasy-skirt Alice were folding
themselves into a love-parcel on a bright June afternoon at the
east end of the precinct, right under crooked Charlie's brand-new
chapel-scaffold, the whole damn lot had come down on top of
'em, two ton of it if it was an ounce.

ALICE. For he's throwing up them chapel wallstones like Babel in the
Bible, all but crippled my poor Sam for life. They sent him here to
the York garrison, his arm and leg like — *withered* — all he's good for
is to keep the captain's quarters for him, hobble in and out of town
with the odd message — eh, Nick love, my poor Sam, he wor the
best bloody cross-bow shooter in the whole of his company! He's
your crazy Charlie to thank for the state he's in now. Do you know
two of Charlie's journeymen wor killed when the scaffold came
down?

NICK (*in horror*). *Killed!* And I must have known 'em: who were they?

ALICE. Nay, you'd not have known 'em, Nick. His old gang have all
left him, they wouldn't bide on the job. So he's fetched in
workmen as mad as himself from God knows where across the
mountains, Scots even, some of 'em. They say the devil lays stone
for him after dark when they're all in bed, on account he made a
hellfire bargain for it.

NICK. Ah, they say that of any mason where the work goes more
brisk than is usual.

ALICE. It could be true, though, with Charlie. That Frenchwoman he
wed with is witchcraft, you know, makes spells for him on
parchment: it's true, I've seen his prentices trying to study them
on the work-gantry. Eh, Nick, you had a lucky escape there.

NICK. Spells . . . ?

> (*Speaking as narrator*). Now I knew it wouldn't be spells. What
> it was, of course, this famous mystery the dead Frenchman passed
> on to her. Could Charlie Bones be really fool enough to let his
> lads get their ignorant hands on it, though? Aye and he could, if
> he'd lost his head in all the clamour of the new contract: I'd known
> him lose his wild black head, time and again, when things got
> turbulent. Secret science . . . aye, Charlie's crafty: but I'd say he
> was far from wise.

> (*To* ALICE). Alice, hinny, you've brought me tidings: I've a notion
> they ought to be looked into.

ALICE. I thought you'd think that.

NICK. Wait though, this soldier o'yourn, Sam, all but crippled, did you
say? I know you make no claim on my good nature, but —

The sound of money passed over. And a kiss.

ALICE (*emotionally*). Eh, Nick, you're a good man, you deserve
better nor you've gained: but I reckon they won't give it you . . .

NICK. They might, if damfool Charlie's broadcasting all he's been
taught. All but finished now, that barbican. Wait while the hard
weather's had out its worst: and then back north: to discover.

Scene Eleven

*Fade in the sounds of work on a building site, clink of masons' hammers,
banging of carpenters' tools, calling of men from scaffolds, etc. This is
on the Minster Hill: an impression of height — rooks calling, wind blowing,
perhaps.*

CHARLIE (*in between the clink of his chisel*). No: I've not time.
There's another six of these arch centrings to be rounded out with
stone afore the hard weather comes down on us again, this
sunshine's deceptive, it'll be over and gone by the week's end.
Tell the Prior I've not got time to have words with him now.

YOUNG PRENTICE (*in a Scots accent*). You'll never send a message
the like o'that to the Prior. He'll have you off the job with a
criss-cross-Jesus-bless-me without a moment to wash your fingers.
Hoo!

CHARLIE. Not tonight he won't, for you won't bloody tell him
tonight: leave it till morning, you can't find me: right then, get out
of my road.

The PRENTICE *is heard walking off along the scaffold.*

CHARLIE (*speaking to himself obsessively as he works*). No, I was too
slow, too slow as always that time: if it'd been left up to me I'd have

lost both wife and job. *She* was the speedy one, outpacing both me and Nick Squinch. I might well ha' lost all of it, never again, never again too slow, Charlie, Prior's message or no message . . .

Fade out.

Scene Twelve

Similar building noises: but we are on the ground now. Hasty footsteps — sandals flapping on stone pavement.

PRIOR (*calling impatiently*). Master Charles, are you up there?

PRIOR'S CLERK (*also calling*). Master Charles, it's the Father Prior!

CHARLIE (*from close to*). I'm not up, I'm down here. 'Morning, sir, we're pressed with work. (*He calls.*) MacHarl, are you up there?

YOUNG PRENTICE (*from a distance*). Aye aye?

CHARLIE. You can set in the keystone for the last arch now! I'll be with you in five minutes to see how it's done!

YOUNG PRENTICE (*from a distance*). It'll be done, master, as crisp as your eggs and bacon!

CHARLIE (*to himself*). Damn that, she gave me nowt but cold gruel yet again . . . (*Aloud*). Now sir: er, your reverence, sir.

PRIOR (*containing himself with an effort*). Twelve pillars, Master Charles? According to the agreed contract there should be nine, three rows of three?

CHARLIE. I believe so, sir, yes. It'll cost you no more, you know.

PRIOR. I suppose not. The columns, I observe, are considerably attenuated. Quite different from those in the choir.

PRIOR'S CLERK. To which your work was to conform, if I remember the agreement.

CHARLIE (*resentful and defensive*). Now sir, *I* remember it, every detail notched clear on a tally-stick of wood and marked with the Lord Bishop's seal. I have my half of the tally, under lock and key in the lodge. Do you want I should get it out?

PRIOR. Not necessary. As it seems you are fully prepared to admit your unauthorised variations. It *has* been suggested you are attempting an embezzlement.

CHARLIE (*thunderstruck*). What?

PRIOR. You estimate a certain quantity of wrought stone, build with but half of it, and pocket the cost of the remainder.

CHARLIE (*not sure whether to take this seriously or not*). Oh, aye, and you think that that's likely?

PRIOR. I do not. You are not so foolish as to believe you could do it and avoid detection. But there must be some reason. Just look at it: attenuated, meagre, devoid altogether of solidity and the majesty of God: to be frank this work resembles the bars of a birdcage. Your predecessor from France —

PRIOR'S CLERK. — whose sad loss we so largely lament —

PRIOR. He would never have perpetrated such a — such a —

CHARLIE (*still resentful: but speaking with great earnestness*). Because he never had instruction to build a house for the Queen of Heaven, that's why. Look up there, to the west of us, the bulk of that great minster — his dream, and he shaped it. And I'm not that much younger than he was, the time the full dream of it came into his mind, but I am, by so many years, advanced further forward, toward the coming again of Christ, trump of judgement, end of all things, perfection. D'you know what I mean?

PRIOR'S CLERK. At the very least you must mean a most monstrous impertinence —

PRIOR. More than that: he means heresy.

CHARLIE (*furious that he is not understood*). No, reverence, no, I speak only of my own dream for the new shape of the new chapel, for Our Lady, it is *Her work*, reverence —

PRIOR. It is certainly not *your* work any longer. You are dismissed, Master Charles. and think yourself fortunate you are not also bound in chains.

A pause.

CHARLIE (*very slowly, controlling his immediate emotions*). Do I take it, sir, you believe there is matter here of breach-of-contract?

PRIOR'S CLERK. Never mind what you take or do not take: you are dismissed. The Prior has said.

CHARLIE (*ignoring him*). Because if that is so, sir: I make immediate appeal to the Lord Bishop. Master to talk to Master. *His* seal on *my* contract.

PRIOR. You know very well the Lord Bishop determined *me* to administer contracts.

CHARLIE. Aye aye: but if they *are* broke, it's his loss and not yours. Sir, I make appeal.

Fade out.

Scene Thirteen

The sound of sandalled feet pacing in a cloister. Gregorian chant heard from a distance.

PRIOR. Did you not yet find out, Brother, how that scaffold collapsed last June?

PRIOR'S CLERK. I can get no better story than it had been loosened in the night of the great wind: the men who went up the next day had taken drink — some of his Scotsmen, Reverend Father — they failed to ensure that the supports were —

PRIOR. Yes . . . Did I mistake, or was there a woman up there on the gantry today?

PRIOR'S CLERK. His wife, Reverend Father.

PRIOR. Ah? She brings him his dinner, I suppose?

PRIOR'S CLERK. He brings his own dinner, a piece of cold turnip, or something of that, in the pocket of his gown. No, Reverend Father, she is not a woman for dinner. And yet she is upon the work any hour of the day she cares to choose. She governs him, the men say.

PRIOR. But this is an impropriety, why was I not told?

PRIOR'S CLERK. The dedication of the chapel, to Our Lady, the workmen think that she brings them good fortune: she has, like the Lord Bishop, a special devotion, I believe —

PRIOR (*sharply*). No! I told the Lord Bishop this dedication was not wise. Our Blessed Saint Cuthbert avoided all women at all times, he bore in mind the first Eve, the shameless nudity of her crime against the bliss of Mankind. Why, his most sacred shrine, with his holy bones within it, lies but a few yards from the very entry to this new chapel. He cannot but be *conturbed* in the austerity of his last resting-place. Our simple brethren may even believe his distressed spirit cast down the scaffold last summer as a warning to us all.

PRIOR'S CLERK. I wish I could persuade myself that the frenzy of Master Charles for reducing size and weight of structure had nothing to do with it.

PRIOR. That too, of course: but if so, his foolishness was but an instrument for Blessed Cuthbert's aroused judgement. See that that woman comes no more upon the building-site. You may tell her why. She can practise her devotion elsewhere. I do wish the Bishop would. I must speak to him. Besides, if this mutinous man insists upon appealing to him —

PRIOR'S CLERK. I don't think the Lord Bishop will trouble himself with that. He is far too much embroiled with his large responsibilities. I am sure that your decision will stand, Reverend Father . . .

Scene Fourteen

BISHOP'S CLERK. No, of course you can't see the Bishop. The Lord Bishop has made known to you his needs and requirements. Administrative difficulty, apply to the Prior: financial, apply to the Treasurer.

CHARLIE. Sir, it's nowt to do with money, there's money enough laid forward, I've no hesitation there, sir. Oh no, sir, I'm talking now, sir, of a concern about my personal honour.

BISHOP'S CLERK. Nonsense, you are an artisan: do you take yourself for a captain-of-horse? Be off with you, fulfil your function.

Scene Fifteen

Fade in a boy's voice singing 'Salve Regina'. The music comes to an end. A pair of hands, softly clapping.

BISHOP. Thank you, thank you. What a very sweet child, and how beautifully he hymns the grace of Our Blessed Lady. How old are you, child? . . . Ha, we are shy. Such beautiful soft hair, curls of a considerate sweet-natured angel, and the voice angelic too. See that someone gives him a sugar-plum, or two, or three, before he returns to the choir . . . You were saying?

BISHOP'S CLERK. His personal honour! Such wanton incontinent aspiration, and the mortar and lime in a crust all over his boots.

BISHOP. But you tell me he was distressed?

BISHOP'S CLERK. In a brute passion, My Lord, it seemed.

BISHOP. Perhaps we should have seen him. Some uncouth demon shaking a rake through the labyrinth of his bowels. Which could portend disturbance in the conduct of the work. A new house for Our Lady must derive before all else from delighted souls in harmony.

BISHOP'S CLERK. From your own soul, I suppose, My Lord, wherein the work was first conceived —

BISHOP. Suppose nothing of the sort, sir, if you please. This turbulent diocese, and moreover the King's business which I must handle for him toward the Scots, they entirely abolish any harmony in *my* soul. I think we may very well have to muster troops for another war . . . And remember it is not *me* who must hand-by-hand erect this chapel. We are talking of half-shaped men, these craftsmen, Christian men, oh yes, and of keen bodily skill: but ignorant, unlettered, incapable to place their passions, as we do, my dear son, according to the rigorous latinity and logic of the schools. Ask the Prior, if you please, to let me know what is going on.

BISHOP'S CLERK. My Lord . . .

BISHOP. And now, shall we have a look at the financial returns from our coal-mines? It ought to be possible to ship these combustible stones to London, we could make quite a profit for the diocese, don't you think . . . and a great name as a mercantile innovator? Our celebrity for majestic building-work is already assured, yes?

Scene Sixteen

DAUGHTER (*as narrator*). So after all Saint Cuthbert would not have my polluted womb so close to his bones: I am ordered off the work, with of course not a gesture of courtesy. I can't object, or they would wonder why. If they did wonder why, they might go so far as to find out — what, Arabian mathematic, Judaean instruction in it — "oho, to a pile of fire for that one — !" If the Lord God gets wind of me when I come to His last judgement, He too might be ordering some fire. They say, if it is *His* fire, it will never go cold. But we do have a stratagem against Him.

Obtain a sly protection in the lobby of the court
From the Mother of His Son,
O Lady avert the consequence!
Through You alone it can be done.
Your bright new house,
Twelve pillars of slim stone,
Take it, my bribe and offering,
Let it atone . . .

And yet, if I am never allowed there, how can I assure myself that he is building it true? I warned him about that scaffold, but he left it to his untrained Scotsmen, and it fell. Their own fault, in a way, but they cast the blame on Charlie, and now he blames me for it. Lady Mary I do believe he was glad to see me ordered away from his work. For now it has become *his* work, the pride of his own power, no-one else's. If he completes it without disaster, he will rear himself over me to the height of King Nimrod! And Our Lady will hate him: she will hate the chapel he has built in Her name: and, of course, she will hate *me*. So, therefore, do I want, that all his workmanship should fail . . . ? Oh . . . Oh . . . She did say, 'Put down the mighty from their seat'. If only I did not think that that might include *me* . . . But it did *not* include me. Because Nick Squinch came back from York, and who but She could have fetched him?

NICK (*outside*). Nay come on, open up, we're not old enemies yet, just for two cross words at a good-bye.

DAUGHTER. My husband is not here.

NICK (*with a laugh — outside*). Of course he's not, he's haunting the Bishop, I found that out before I came.

DAUGHTER (*as narrator*). I could not resist his laughter. I opened the door. He took me in his arms.

The door opens.

NICK. So, the Prior took offence they tell me at the innovations of Charlie's structure.

DAUGHTER. The beauty of his structure.

NICK. Yours, I suppose, more than his?

DAUGHTER. Indeed no: his.

NICK. I'm glad of that: because there's a crack you could put your fist through; top-to-bottom of the south cross-wall of that Lady Chapel: the weight of stone above his first four arches —

DAUGHTER. It can't be true!

NICK. I've just been there, I've just seen it: it only appeared this morning. His young Scotchmen are all stood gaping at it like a herd of stranded porpoises, asking one another who'll dare to break the news to him . . . Eh, Lord, she's fainted a swoon.

DAUGHTER (*in an agony*). No, it cannot be *my* fault —

NICK. I suppose it can. You could have forewarned him.

DAUGHTER. But I did I did I did — oh judgement, the mighty pulled down!

NICK (*as narrator*). Why, she writhed herself round and about like a viper in a hot oven — that much of her in grief and fear, that much of her in towering joy — I said to her, 'make up your mind' —

(*Speaking to her*). Make up your mind, child, do we save him or let him ruin?

DAUGHTER (*in a despair*). Whichever way, it is *my* ruin — my crab-trap bed was made and now I must lie in it and welter. Charlie Bones was like my father: he built Jerusalem in his dirty sleep: and now forever I must sleep with *him*. It is my punishment.

NICK (*as narrator*). I understood well enough what for.

(*Speaking to her*). It *was* you loosed the scaffold underneath the Frenchman's foot, wasn't it? Made a murder so your forbidden knowledge could be transferred where you chose. But you chose wrong.

DAUGHTER. You will inform against me? Send me to death?

NICK. Eh dear, hinny, no, I'd never do a thing like that. That wolf-hearted dad of yourn was the greatest in the northern guild, *revered:* by all them as never had to suffer him. To let the world hear the full manner of his death would let fly a sight too much of the manner of his life — what'd the clergy do towards us all then, that jealous of the craft as you know they've been, always? Besides, we've to think of his secrets, the mystery of his art — oh aye, I've been hearing stories. You go to death, girl, all o' that goes likewise: lost for ever, no good to anyone? That chapel is a fair master's-piece: I'd give anything to have known of the science that would have enabled me build it myself. If *I'd* built it, it'd never have cracked. You know, sweetheart, I think it's time you and me contrived some *sharing* . . . Sit close now, close to Nick, that's right, down here, on your sheepskin . . .

Scene Seventeen

CHARLIE (*as narrator*). It seemed this time the Bishop had had thoughts, gave instructions, I was admitted. He had the Prior with him, savage. Of course they kept me at the long end of the room, I couldn't hear what they said to each other, save for fragments. He walked about among his choirboys, stroking their young necks.

The sound of boys' voices singing the 'Salve Regina'. Phrases of conversation break in and out among the singing.

BISHOP. To my conjecture, Father Prior, he is possessed by the beauty of holiness . . . words of stone, not words of mouth, he can't articulate *those* . . .

PRIOR. But to talk to your clerk of his personal honour —

BISHOP. The honour of Our Lady . . .

PRIOR. But, Blessed Cuthbert . . .

BISHOP. Your saint, not mine, you were born in this drear country, I was not. But I think that he must be allowed to fulfil the work — naturally there should be some financial increment . . . Father Prior, *we desire it.* You may go.

The sound of sandalled feet slapping the tiled floor and a door slams.

BISHOP. You heard that, master mason?

CHARLIE (*as narrator*). I hadn't, of course, but I guessed when the Prior walked out. He fetched me near and repeated. I was to be kept on the work, and my wages went up!

He gives a great shout, as he runs along a vaulted passage.

CHARLIE. Ha ha *ha!!* Charlie and nowt but Charlie to carry the crown of the craft for ever!!!

His running feet stop short, and his shout. He speaks again as narrator.

Young MacHarl at the end of the passage: he was in search for me to tell me: about the crack in the cross-wall . . . Self-murder is a terrible

sin. So I chose not to venture it . . . Instead: I went down home.
Oh God . . . Nick Squinch upon the hearth-stone with my
wife? There are some murders are no sin. I had a great chisel at once
in my hand: but —

Scene Eighteen

*The sound of a brief struggle, a cry from the French daughter, a gasp
from* NICK, *a yell of pain from* CHARLIE, *a chisel falls to the floor.*

CHARLIE (*as narrator*). But he being a man of good strong body — one
leap from him, one kick — it left me a broken crab-shell thrown
against my own house-wall. Top-to-bottom you could put your
whole fist into the riven midst of my life.

(*Speaking to her — in pain*). You told me, you shifty bitch, the
proportions of that wall were exact!

DAUGHTER. I told you Nick Squinch would have had an opinion.
Well, he has. You'd better listen to it.

NICK. Charlie, I've had a short, but very deep, look at that wall of
yourn, Charlie. It could have stood, if you'd taken thought. No
more nor a foot or two here in the placing of stone, change of
weight there. It can still stand. Question is, will the clergymen let it?

CHARLIE. Not at my hands, not any more. I'm disgraced: and the
whole dream of my columns and arches, disgraced.

NICK. If they disgrace you, they disgrace your good wife: and Nick
Squinch has a warmth towards her —

DAUGHTER (*as narrator*). She's not at all sure any more she has a
warmth toward Nick but who could deny a man that holds her
life at his mercy . . . ?

NICK. More than that though, they'd disgrace the guild: we must all
gang together to protect one another's mistakes, or the clergy
will rule us for always. Now, Charlie: your old mate Nick by strange
chance this unfortunate day is the only master in town with
experience of work on the minster fabric. I've no doubt the Father
Prior will be in search of an expert survey, a report upon the damage
to your wall . . .

CHARLIE (*as narrator*). Betwixt the pair of 'em, on my damned
hearth-stone they put together the crafty play to help Nick Squinch
to save my life for me. God I wish I had murdered them both.

Scene Nineteen

*Fade in the creaking of feet on ladders and scaffold. Birds, wind etc. . . .
but no tools heard.*

PRIOR'S CLERK. His columns were far too slender, Master Nicholas,
do you not agree?

Some tapping at the stones as they examine them.

NICK. At first sight, I'd not have thought so.

PRIOR. Not? But it surely is beyond dispute that —

NICK. Of course it'll all have to come down. Strip it to the foundation . . .
Eh, dear: it's an odd thing. Weight of wall on these piers ought easily
to have been carried . . .

PRIOR. Are you sure? You stand there peering downward like a man
in a trance.

NICK. Strange . . .

PRIOR. *What* is strange? Collect yourself, articulate. (*Aside to* CLERK.)
Of course, he can't, they never can: that's exactly the difficulty . . .

NICK (*in dream-like speech*). They come up, d'you see from downwards,
up through the wall, two, three — no, five — reaching cracks, like
the fingers of a huge black hand, as it were, like, from down below,
and from this side, down below, *there* . . .

PRIOR (*disturbed*). What does he mean? He speaks as though it
were — something not natural . . . ?

PRIOR'S CLERK. Master Nicholas! Master Nicholas, do you tell the
Prior this is *not* according to the order of a regular fault in masonry?

Scene Twenty

BISHOP. Clearly the good man is extremely superstitious.

PRIOR. You yourself said, My Lord, 'words of stone, not words of
mouth', 'half-shaped men'; if he believes the devil's hand is stretching
out of hell to drag down the good work, then he believes it: and
they all will.

BISHOP. Already two men killed last year, and the last master-mason,
the Frenchman, what happened to him? Father Prior, we can't have
the devil prevailing against our own fabric!

BISHOP'S CLERK. We could exorcise, My Lord.

BISHOP. Nonsense, from an entire minster? The very fact of the
ceremonial would make it seem the powers of darkness had a victory
here already.

PRIOR'S CLERK (*greatly daring*). My Lord, *I* think the chapel has
been incompetently built . . .

BISHOP. It probably has, yes: and with sufficient extra strengthening —
not too much, lest we mar the elegance — I'm sure we could
re-build. But on the same part of the site, with such an opinion
running round among the workmen? Indeed on *any* part of the
site —

BISHOP'S CLERK. We could transfer the same design to the *west*
end — unusual for a Lady Chapel, but —

BISHOP. But we would need to explain why the *west* end should be
immune from more interference by the devil . . . It is not always
undesirable that the artisans have these strange beliefs. A
masoncraft that holds only to its own mechanic science would very
soon slide away from dependence upon the Church. Men would
build for their own glory, not the glory of God. So think of a good
reason for the west end to be immune from the devil's hand,
think of one . . .

PRIOR (*suddenly excited*). Why indeed, My Lord, I have it! Oh yes,
a huge hand, but indeed not the devil's hand! Blessed Cuthbert!
My Lord, a miracle . . . !

Scene Twenty-One

PRIOR'S CLERK (*as narrator*). So: into the Minster Chronicle, I take
my pen and write. 'Every stone that the workmen set up for the
chapel was most marvellously cast down and could not be re-erected.
This at the hand of Blessed Saint Cuthbert, who willed not that his
severe retirement in the privacy of his tomb be scandalously
infected by the passage of women into a sanctuary hard by, where
their devotions would have been beyond remedy continuous. All
of which being revealed to the Father Prior in an inspired dream,
it was determined to convey the Lord Bishop's new chapel to the
west end of the Minster, and so build it without hindrance, as
was in the upshot most conveniently achieved. Praise to the holy
saint for his miracle, wherewith his famous shrine has been
copiously adorned by the consequent offerings of the faithful. Much
fame has thereby ensued for the masons and craftsmen of the land:
their prayers ascend to heaven in gratitude for all these wonders . . .'

Scene Twenty-Two

CHARLIE (*as narrator*). The Prior's Clerk did recommend Nick Squinch
take charge of the new work at the west end. But Nick Squinch,
in regard for the reputation of us all, told the Prior that bad luck
and ill-feeling would breed among the guild if any such change were

to be made. So Nick Squinch took a look at my load-bearing measurements, increased them, decreased them, where needed: and this time the walls stayed put. No less beautiful than before — like, in France they now build that slender, you could believe churches made of reeds and bulrush, three parts flying through the air . . . !

Scene Twenty-Three

DAUGHTER (*as narrator*). Will my father come and haunt me because now his occult science belongs to Nick as well as Charlie, and thereafter through their prentices to every master in the northern guild? So far he has made no sign . . . the Virgin keeps him away from me. Or perhaps he does haunt me, in the shape of Nick — perhaps the Virgin —

NICK (*as narrator*). Perhaps the Virgin, so gratified with the grace and privacy of Her bright new house, has wrought a miracle to turn a dead man's vengeance into a live man's midnight visiting?

(*He speaks to her*). It's all right, hinny, Charlie Bones keeps the dark hours on his scaffold-gantry, watching and brooding over the work. It's all right, he has no real need for any wife, beyond the work, and we both know that. You and me, now, quiet and warm —

DAUGHTER. Oh as quiet as an easy conscience . . . (*They laugh a little together*.) I thought you came here so I could teach you mathematic.

NICK (*suggestively*). So I did and so you're going to. But there's more ways than one to put this, and that, together: let's take the easiest first . . .

DAUGHTER (*as narrator*). He is content, after all, to let Charlie carry the crown of the craft, so long as Charlie sleeps alone, and I am well content for that. The old holy man also, horrid Cuthbert in his ancient bitterness, he too can now rejoice in the loneliness of his jealous bed . . .

Scene Twenty-Four

Fade in wind and sea sounds out of which grows CUTHBERT's *voice as in Scene One.*

CUTHBERT.
  They bring me jewels, they bring me gold,
  Embroidered cloth they do unfold:
  Piled up above my box of wood.
  Such gauds and glory, oh I would not wear
  Their vain adornings even if I could.
  Such lies they tell themselves about my life:

How do they know I do not seek a wife
Here in the tomb in chill and gloom?
Let *them* come down, and they might find
The longings of a dead man's mind
More strange by far than ever they could foretell . . .
Where is the soft brown cow? Her hooves, her horns, her tail?
She led me here and no-one thinks of her.
And yet, and yet, her haunches still will stir.

The lowing of the cow arises from among the noises of the sea, loud enough to overcome them for a moment.

Fade out.

HOOPOE DAY

by Harry Barton

To Marjorie

Harry Barton was born in Belfast. He left the Royal Navy as a captain in 1967. For many years he was an outside contributor to *Punch*. Once a week, 1970-1976, he broadcast in Ulster the letters he received from a Mr Mooney, diehard PRO of the Queen's Own Loyal Sinn Fein Republican Volunteers. His Young Puffin, *Sponge, X and Y,* is soon to have a Japanese edition. His plays include *A Borderline Case* (Dublin Festival 1975); *The Giant Lobelia* (Dublin Festival 1976); *Kelly's Book* (Belfast Festival 1982;shortly to be recorded for Radio Telefis Eireann) and *Pinocchio* (New University of Ulster's Riverside Theatre 1981). *Hoopoe Day* has also been transmitted by Radio Telefis Eireann and the stage version was first presented in Belfast. Harry Barton was awarded the OBE in January 1983 for his work as Chairman of the Northern Ireland Unesco Committee. He and his wife live in the west of Ulster. They like gardening, bird-watching and travel and they have two sons and a grandson.

Hoopoe Day was first broadcast on BBC Radio 3 on 5th October 1982. The cast was as follows:

NICHOLAS, *eight-five, ornithologist*   Christopher Casson
MARIA, *sixty, his niece*   Doreen Hepburn
WILL, *sixty, ornithologist*   Aiden Grennell
GEORGE, *Maria's dead husband* }
ANOTHER ORNITHOLOGIST   }   Maurice O'Callaghan

Director: Robert Cooper

The call of the hoopoe. The word is pronounced 'Hoopoo'. The bird is so called because of the sound it makes: a 'rapid far-carrying clipped Hoo-poo-poo.'
The main room of NICHOLAS's *house.*

NICHOLAS (*to himself*). The call of the hoopoe. I hear it so clearly in my head.

The call of the hoopoe.

NICHOLAS (*to* MARIA, *lifting his voice*). This day week, on 4th May, Maria, I shall be eighty-five years old, and on that day I shall hear a hoopoe calling. Maria. Are you listening?

MARIA (*to herself*). He bothers me. Sitting there, that scrawny profile. Every day he's more tense. Intent and staring.

NICHOLAS. Thus alerted, I shall grip my field glasses and watch the garden: the lawn and the cherry tree, and beyond the lawn, the rose hedge.

MARIA (*to herself*). Ten years he's been there, in that chair, at that great window.

NICHOLAS. The cherry blossom will still be with us this day week, but the white and scented roses of the hedge will not have appeared. I shall watch the lawn in particular. Hoopoes like lawns. To feed they thrust their long curved bills into the turf. My hoopoe will do that. You hear me, Maria?

MARIA (*to herself*). I don't like certitude. Dogmatists have it. 'The Virgin Mary did not die like other people. Instead, she floated upwards. You understand me? Floated upwards.' And my poor dead George's certitude. It's worse if you love the owner of the certitude.

She walks across with a tray and sets it down.

MARIA (*to* NICHOLAS). Scrambled eggs, glass of wine, digestive biscuits.

NICHOLAS. You were there behind me?

MARIA. I can be wraith-like when I choose.

NICHOLAS. Eggs and wine. I welcome the smell. Every evening.

MARIA (*matter-of-fact; she is never cosy*). You're not exacting, I
will say that. I prefer old uncles who are not exacting.

NICHOLAS. This day week, on 4th May, I shall be eighty-five years old
and on that day I shall hear a hoopoe calling.

MARIA (*lightly*). It'll be a nice birthday present.

NICHOLAS. Having heard him, I shall then see him. On the lawn.
(*He drinks.*) He will emerge from among the prickly stems of the
hedge. He will look round sharply, and then stab the turf with his
bill.

MARIA. He could come and have a piece of the birthday cake. Spear
a currant out of it.

NICHOLAS. Maria, I'm telling you. From this window — from this
wheelchair — I have now seen 107 different kinds of birds. They're
all recorded in my old notebook here. (*He eats.*) The hoopoe will
be No. 108.

MARIA. I'd rather see a fat pelican. Flying into Ulster from San
Francisco Bay. I'd like to see him waddle through the garden, his
bill as big as himself.

NICHOLAS. Maria, you're being obstinate. We get all sorts of birds in
this garden, and we are going to get the hoopoe. This February, there
was the lone waxwing. He sat in the cherry tree, high up on the
right-hand side, for two hours. He would fly across my front, remove
a berry from the cotoneaster, and return it to the tree, to the same
perch.

MARIA. Nicholas! A waxwing's a possible —

NICHOLAS. The sealing-wax red in his wing matched the red of the
berry.

MARIA. A waxwing's a possible. We both know that. Here in the
west of Ulster, we're not far beyond the western edge of its range.
But a *hoopoe!* A hoopoe on your *birthday!*

NICHOLAS. It'll be a Hoopoe Day. To see a hoopoe makes any
day special. Do you remember your first one?

MARIA. You know I do. Fifty years ago. Fifty years! I was ten years
old. I remember pointing.

NICHOLAS. You squeaked, and then you pointed.

MARIA. The pink head and the long bill; the crest like an open fan; the
black-and-white bars of the wings. I remember your telling me how
smelly they were.

NICHOLAS. You refused to believe a bird so beautiful could be so smelly.

MARIA. But that was south of Bordeaux. Anyone can find a hoopoe south of Bordeaux.

NICHOLAS. Rubbish dump birds. Lovely, smelly rubbish dump birds. Poking about among the rubbish.

A distant call of the hoopoe.

NICHOLAS. I can almost hear him already, a week ahead of time.

A distant call of the hoopoe.

NICHOLAS. I shall draw him to me out of the air.

Pause.

MARIA (*sharply*). Eat up, now. Gulp your red wine.

NICHOLAS (*eating and drinking*). In the old days, I could always get to the bird I wanted to see. I could go to Sri Lanka for the Ceylon Blue Magpie. I'd know where it might be seen and I'd go and see it, a lizard for its young in its red bill.

MARIA. That's something I'd like to see.

NICHOLAS. But nowadays it's the birds that have to come to me; and the air is full of them, after all, rare vagrants blown from their proper course or home. If I require a hoopoe — and I do require one — he'll come.

MARIA. Sniffing the birthday cake from afar.

NICHOLAS (*spelling it out*). The hoopoe, over the years, has been seen and recorded in twenty-seven of the thirty-two counties of Ireland. Only twenty miles from here there's a man who's been brought one with a broken wing.

MARIA. What will you do if your bird doesn't come? (*Pause.*) What shall you do if you stare at the garden all your long birthday and see no hoopoe?

NICHOLAS (*in flat and humourless certitude*). The bird will come. I shall hear him call.

A distant call of the hoopoe.

NICHOLAS. And then I shall see him.

MARIA. I'll take your tray and leave your glass.

NICHOLAS. He'll float in low over the hedge. He'll land on the lawn. He'll fold his wings and there he'll be. Motionless.

She removes the tray.

MARIA. Shall I top up your glass?

NICHOLAS. No thank you. But leave the note-book.

MARIA. I think I'll go out. For an hour. An hour and a half, maybe.

NICHOLAS. Look at that willow warbler — fussing along the hedge. All the way from Africa every year. Silly little bugger.

MARIA. Nicholas. Are you listening? I'm off out for a time.

She opens the door.

NICHOLAS (*absently*). Take your field glasses or you may miss something.

The door closes as MARIA leaves the room with the tray. Silence.
The sounds of the countryside as heard from inside a call box. A door opens. MARIA enters, dials, listens to ringing and pips, puts money in.

WILL (*distant*). Hallo?

MARIA. Hallo Will? It's Maria here.

WILL (*distant*). So it is. 'Sixty-year-old widower, ornithologist with tidy beard, seeks sincere non-smoking female with a view to matrimony.'

MARIA. What I seek is your hoopoe. Have you let it go yet?

WILL (*at other end*). Not yet, but it'll be any day now. You *seek* it?

MARIA. If I walk south along the road, will you pick me up?

WILL (*at the other end*). I will.

MARIA. And give me a half of lager?

WILL (*at the other end*). I will. I can afford it. I'm index-linked, remember? (*Fading.*) It's a point in my favour.

The sounds of a quiet saloon bar.

MARIA. Lager suits me.

WILL. I like to watch you drinking beer. You drink as though you'd earned it. Which you always have.

MARIA. It was the certitude in the old man's voice: the certitude of dogma. 'God made the world in the year 4004 BC'.

WILL. 'On the twenty-third of January of that year.'

MARIA. 'A Tuesday it was.'

WILL. 'Just after breakfast.'

They laugh; they're pleased to find they share this attitude.

The terrorists have it too.

MARIA. Oh yes, the terrorists.

WILL. 'You are wrong to be upset when I mutilate your baby brother. It is my duty to the cause.'

MARIA (*with a shudder*). Exactly. (*She drinks.*) He reminded me — and I love the old man, you understand — he reminded me of my husband, my late husband, George. He sat month after month in that Home, knitting scarves. Ceaselessly knitting. He only ever said one thing, and he said it with dull and absolute conviction. He would look up as I came in:

GEORGE'S VOICE. It is my duty to knit.

MARIA. I heard that same voice today. 'The hoopoe will come.'

WILL. What happened to all the knitting?

MARIA. Uh?

WILL. All those scarves. What happened to them?

MARIA. I never heard. I wouldn't have wanted them. They might have brought something with them.

WILL. I once met your old uncle, you know.

MARIA. You did? That's really interesting.

WILL. At least a hundred years ago.

MARIA. I don't know why I haven't shown him to you. An elderly diffidence, perhaps —

WILL. I'd enjoy meeting him again. He was scrupulous. He and another ornithologist took a group of us students bird-watching down in Cork. We liked him. He was scrupulous, not to show the world how scientific he was, but because he liked to know about birds. I didn't take to the other man. He'd learned all the bird books by heart and he liked you to know it. That wouldn't have mattered, but he went on from there. He saw birds the rest of us didn't see. Or said he did. He saw them when no one else was there.

Fade out the sound of the saloon bar and fade up estuary sounds, including curlew, black-tailed godwit, oystercatcher and redshank.

One evening, your uncle and I were down on the estuary. A pale evening; low tide. I was looking through the telescope, moving from bird to bird, checking. Redshanks, curlews, oystercatchers, godwits. This man came up behind us: this — this ornithologist.

ORNITHOLOGIST. Ah, there you are. Hidden away. Nicholas. You'd never guess, but I've just seen bee eaters.

NICHOLAS (*explosively*). Bee eaters? Where?

ORNITHOLOGIST. Passing overhead. Three of them. Unmistakeable. The projecting tail feathers. Very familiar. And I heard the flight-note. I'll add them to our List, all right? (*Fading*.) But keep an eye open; you might get a sighting of your own.

NICHOLAS (*to himself*). Bastard. (*To* WILL.) Will, did you believe that?

WILL. Well . . .

NICHOLAS. Come on. Don't be a bashful student. Say what you think.

Pause.

WILL. I don't think he saw a bee-eater — (*excited*) — but I'll tell you what *I* can see, what I've got in this telescope. What I think I've got in this telescope. Come and look. I've not seen one before.

They change places.

NICHOLAS. Ah yes. I see the bird. And you think it's a what?

WILL. A *black*-tailed — not a bar-tailed — a black-tailed godwit.

NICHOLAS. A *black*-tailed godwit? Let me peer at it a moment. The light's odd. It's not only the tail that's different; there's the size . . . Yes. Yes. You're right. A black-tailed godwit. And you hadn't seen one before?

WILL. No.

NICHOLAS. Longer legs, longer bill. Yes. And there'd be the wing-bar in flight. You hadn't seen it but you knew what it should look like.

WILL. Yes.

NICHOLAS. There's hope for you yet. Here, take your telescope.

They change places.

WILL. Handsome, that's what he is. I can't see the wingbar.

NICHOLAS. You'd see it in flight. You've seen a black-tailed godwit. But that bastard didn't see a bee-eater.

WILL. The godwit's not rare.

NICHOLAS. That's not the point.

WILL. There he goes.

NICHOLAS. Can you see the wing bar?

WILL. Yes, a big white wing bar and a big white rump with a black tail bar below it. A handsome, handsome bird.

NICHOLAS. And you saw it. I knew you had before I looked myself. (*Pause*.) It isn't just that the gorgeous bee eater is a rarity in Ireland, the rarest of accidentals. After all, you could see one. It's just that *he* didn't, and I know it. He's at Stage Three.

WILL. Stage Three?

NICHOLAS. And you're at Stage One. Stage One is when you only claim a sighting when you know for sure you've seen the bird. Stage Two is when you begin to give yourself the benefit of the doubt, cheating yourself at patience. Stage Three is the mad certitude. You see a bird in the sky. The word 'bee eater' passes through your head. You've seen a bee eater. Stay in Stage One, Will.

WILL. I certainly shall. I wouldn't be anywhere else.

NICHOLAS. It's not so easy as you think. We're all afraid of Stage Two. Not to mention Stage Three. I certainly am, and always will be. Terrified, sometimes.

WILL. I don't think I believe you.

NICHOLAS. Oh yes, I am. That's why that character makes me wild. Look at him along the shore there, staring into the sky, his binoculars like anti-aircraft guns. Shooting down bee eaters. Gorgeous invisible bloody bee eaters. (*Fading.*) Blue-green, chestnut, black, yellow, and bloody invisible.

The sounds of the saloon bar replaces those of the estuary.

MARIA. He's never resigned himself to that wheel-chair, never.

WILL. All right, then, we'll make sure he really sees his hoopoe.

MARIA. You honestly think we can do it? Are you sure the bird will be fit enough?

WILL. Certain sure. I could almost let him go now.

MARIA. Perhaps you ought to get him south to Bordeaux and let him go there.

WILL. No. I'll put a ring on him and let him go here. He'll know best where to take himself off to.

MARIA. Let's do it, then, and see what happens.

WILL. How'll I know when to release him? I mean, the old man mustn't miss him.

MARIA. You'll be behind the hedge with the bird. He and I will be sitting in the big window. You'll be able to see us. I've checked. When I stand up — that'll be your signal.

WILL (*fading*). OK. The moment you stand up. This day week, the moment you stand up.

Silence. The week passes.

MARIA's *voice, humming 'Happy Birthday to You!' in the main room.*

MARIA. When I get up to fetch the cake, I might miss your hoopoe.

NICHOLAS. You might. But I'll call out. The instant I see him.

MARIA. I'd better risk it then. Eight big candles you'll have, and one little one to bring it to eighty-five.

She pushes her chair back and stands up.

You'll have to blow them out, remember? (*To herself.*) And look, there's the bird, Will's hoopoe, beside the hedge. Standing there bemused by sudden freedom. I'm a magician, and the bird is magic, pink and crested magic. (*To* NICHOLAS, *her excitement real.*) Look, Nicholas! Your hoopoe! Can you see it?

NICHOLAS (*unemotional*). I saw it. I can see it.

MARIA. It stabbed the lawn for a worm. Aren't you — excited?

Pause.

NICHOLAS (*dismissively*). That's not my hoopoe.

MARIA. Not your hoopoe?

NICHOLAS. It's ringed, for one thing.

MARIA. Well, why shouldn't it be ringed? Birds get ringed.

NICHOLAS. It is not my hoopoe.

MARIA. It's your lawn and your hoopoe and your birthday.

NICHOLAS. Someone pushed it through the hedge. It'll be the one that had its wing mended. You were doing me a kindness. And he's enchanting to watch. But it's no matter. My hoopoe — my own hoopoe — will be here in a minute.

MARIA (*to herself*). He makes me shiver. 'My own hoopoe will be here in a minute.'

GEORGE'S VOICE. It is my duty to knit.

MARIA (*to herself*). I want no more of that in this life. (*To* NICHOLAS.) I'll get the cake.

NICHOLAS. I'll call out when it comes.

MARIA *opens the door and closes it behind her. In the kitchen now, she pours from the kettle into the teapot. She strikes a match and lights the candles.*

MARIA (*to herself*). A hoopoe on the lawn and I'm lighting candles.

She opens the door to the main room and closes it behind her. She sets the tray down.

MARIA. Blow out your candles. Take your eyes off that bird for a moment and blow out the candles on your cake.

NICHOLAS. A handsome cake, as always. (*He blows.*)

MARIA. You've missed the little one.

NICHOLAS *blows again.*

MARIA. That's better.

NICHOLAS. Your hoopoe's still there.

MARIA. So it is. Magic. I'll pour.

She pours tea into two cups.

MARIA. And now you'll have to cut the cake. Take your eyes off the window again and cut the . . .

NICHOLAS. Look! My hoopoe's arrived. There are now two hoopoes. Get your glasses on to them. Quick! Get your glasses on to them.

Pause.

MARIA (*to herself*). I can't look. I have the glasses to my eyes, but I daren't look. My shutters are up. Nelson did something like this. If I open my eyes, I'll see — I'll finally see — that the old man, my old and favourite uncle — is mad. I don't want another madness. I wish Will was here in the room. I need sanity. I need it. I'm finished with husbands for ever, mad or sane, but I wish someone was here, I wish Will was here, was up here from behind that hedge. 'Widow, non-smoking and sane, seeks sane ornithologist, preferably with tidy beard.' Lie to the old man quickly, tell him the lie. (*To* NICHOLAS.) Yes, yes, I see them. Both of them. The pink heads. The crests. The black-and-white wings. The two long bills, curving downwards. Yes, yes. All two of them. I do see them. I do.

Pause.

NICHOLAS. And there they go! Off into the sky together! As though they'd known each other all their lives. My hoopoe! Hand me my notebook, Maria, and I'll record them. Bird No. 108. Two of them, one artificially introduced, one a true accidental. Please, Maria, the notebook.

MARIA (*to herself*). Keep your eyes from the window. Open them but keep them away. Avert them, as from a ghost.

NICHOLAS. A true birthday accidental!

MARIA. Here's your book. Here's your pen. (*Pause.*) Go on, write. Write them in. (*Pause. To herself.*) And now what's the matter with him? He's not writing. His hand is shaking. The whole of him is shaking. He's dropped the pen.

The pen hits the floor.

(*To* NICHOLAS.) Nicholas, you've dropped your pen. (*To herself.*) The whole of the old man is shaking.

(*To* NICHOLAS, *aghast*). What is it? Nicholas? Favourite of all uncles? What is it?

NICHOLAS (*whispering*). It's beyond belief. Maria, it's beyond belief.

MARIA. Give me your hand. Of course, it's beyond belief. Bony
old liver-spotted claw! I'll just hold it for you and stop it shaking.
You remember what the man said? If his right hand knew what his
left hand was doing, he'd have to sit on it to keep it from shaking?
I'll just hold it for you. I'll hold them both for you — till next you
need them.

NICHOLAS (*whispering*). I couldn't have seen two. It's beyond belief —
it's beyond belief like that bastard's bee eater, all those years
ago in Cork. You were lying, Maria. As I would be if I made a note
in my book. It's beyond belief, but I caught myself in time. (*He
breathes as though falling asleep.*)

MARIA. That's the way. Close your eyes. They see too much when
they're open. They never stop looking. Close them and rest them.

A long pause. NICHOLAS *breathing.*

I'll tell you something. You saw a hoopoe, in your garden, on your
birthday.

NICHOLAS (*managing a small laugh*). If you have a man down there
behind the hedge with a cageful of hoopoes, why don't you go and
bring him in? (*Fading.*) He could have a piece of the cake.

*Garden bird-song as at the end of May, preferably including willow
warbler's. A tractor in the distance.* MARIA *opens a garden gate.*

MARIA. Will? Are you there? Will?

WILL (*some yards off. He is staring at the sky and speaks without
turning towards* MARIA). Is that you, Maria?

MARIA. Yes?

WILL. Look where I'm looking. That's the way they went.

MARIA. Uh?

WILL. I saw two fly. Did you see two, Maria? Did the old man see
two? I saw two. I saw two hoopoes fly.

Cross-fade to the call of the hoopoe.

INVISIBLE WRITING

by Donald Chapman

For little Emma

Donald Chapman was born in London in 1930. After peripatetic schooling, he spent a brief time in the film industry before studying graphic design. Later he served in the infantry and afterwards wrote and designed for advertising, subsequently moving on to PR, publishing and journalism. He was a staff writer for the *News Chronicle* and later for Associated Newspapers. He has published children's books, poetry and short stories. His award-winning story, *The Hawkmoth in the Garden*, was broadcast in 1977. He is a widower living and working in London and his principal interests lie in the arts, natural history and the human comedy.

Invisible Writing was first broadcast on BBC Radio 4 on 7th July 1982. The cast was as follows:

YOUNG HELEN, *aged 7-14*   Astra Sheridan
HELEN, *aged 14-27*   Sylvestra Le Touzel

Director: Peter King

Whitstable, July 1936

Dear Daddy,

We got here safely and the weather is awful. The landlady is awful
too and she is very mean with the food but you know what Mummy is
like, she won't complain or do anything. I heard the landlady,
Mrs Bowles, say to Mr Bowles, who is her husband, that Mummy will go
too far one of these days. Mr Bowles looked sad. Mrs Bowles has a son
Tony but I don't like him. He is crafty and nosy. He took the pound
you sent to me to buy sweets, he said, but I never got any. He says I only
pretend to be little and am not any more. What does this mean? I am
not a grown-up. My room is at the back so I cannot see the waves. It is
just like home really only you are not here. Are you really coming like
you promised?

I love you, Daddy,
Helen.

Glasgow, April 1937

Dear Mummy,

I hope your head and chest are better and that you are not too sick
in the mornings. Daddy says you ask for it but I know you don't really.
Are you comfortable where you are? Is your new friend any better than
Daddy? Daddy says I drive him mad asking questions all the time but I
never get any answers. Daddy still likes to go out in the evening and
I read and draw and have a cold supper. Tonight I had pigs' trotters and
Daddy is bringing home fish and chips tomorrow. My cat is run over.
I called him Tiny Tim because there was something wrong with him, all
thin and limping. Daddy says it is a good thing.

God bless you Mummy,
Love, Helen

Glasgow, August 1937

Dear Mummy,

    I don't like it here. While there was just Daddy and me it wasn't too
bad but the new lady spoils everything. She is called Mary and she is
very bossy and we don't get on. She won't have my drawings and
painting things in the room or the things I have started to make out of
cardboard. I had a little theatre which she threw on the fire but Daddy
doesn't care. He is soppy about her. He tells me to be a good girl and
won't hear anything against her.

    Mary has got my room to put her things in so now she has two
rooms, Daddy's and mine, and I sleep in the box room with the bear
you bought me.

    Daddy says if you pay the fare I can see you for Christmas since you
mention it in your letter. I hope Jim is nicer than Mary. Would he
take me to a picture gallery?

                        All my love,
                        Helen

Whitstable, June 1938

Dear Daddy,

    I will be nine next month or have you forgotten? I am back here
again with Mummy and the weather is lovely, very calm and warm. We
are here for three weeks. Uncle Jim comes down for the weekend in
a car like yours only a Morris I think.

    On Sunday we went to the harbour which I'm very fond of. When
the tide is out there is all this mud and if you drop a stone in it just
vanishes. There is a squelch sound and it's gone without a trace like
being swallowed. Uncle Jim gave me lots of stones and my arm still
aches.

    I think you would like Uncle Jim and anyway I expect you will
meet him because he is going to marry Mummy.

    I am very happy, Daddy, and hope you are too. Please give my love
to Mary and please answer, you never do.

                        Your affectionate daughter,
                        Helen.

Bromley, September 1939

Dear Uncle Jim,

    Mummy and me miss you very much and hope you will soon be
back with us. Mummy worries all the time but I said at least you
haven't been called up like Daddy. I think she would be calmer if there
wasn't a war but I told her business has to go on war or no war. Is
Lancaster very cold? I don't know why but I see it as cold and damp
and grey. I hope your hotel is cheerful at any rate.

Last week we were issued with gas masks. Very horrible black rubber things with a snout like a big pepper mill. They smell awful and muffle your voice and steam your face up. The bit you see out of mists up too. It lives in a cardboard box with a string handle and I hope I never have to wear it again. There is one for younger children shaped like Mickey Mouse which I think is even more grotesque.

Your garden looks a picture but with all the fruit trees it is more like an orchard. Now that you are my stepfather Mummy thinks I should call you Daddy but I prefer you as Uncle Jim and I know you don't mind. I am a bit concerned about Mummy, not the worrying over you, but herself. She complains of strange feelings. I saw a look of awful fear on her once which frightened me. She won't see a doctor but perhaps you can do something when you come down. It's a pity she has no relatives and is all alone except for you and me. Daddy never writes since that first time.

I think I am getting on quite well with my studies at the Catholic school. I quite like the nuns even though I am not one of theirs. There is an air of almost as if nothing really matters and that suits me. I suppose it's the war. The boys do nothing but paint lead soldiers and you can smell this sticky green paint in class, not unpleasant. They are very cruel to insects I have noticed and keep the heads of poor stag beetles in matchboxes. These heads can still move their pincers and I wondered if it applied to all heads. Do you think the head of Mary Queen of Scots could twitch anything? I made a drawing of Sister Agnes which I am enclosing. Come home soon, Uncle Jim, you are a lovely man.

                    Love, Helen

Bromley, October 1940

Dear Dad,

Thank you for the letter and photo. You are very thin and young-looking — Mummy didn't recognise you! But you are such a long way away. The Burma Road doesn't look a bit like I imagined it. I suppose I was thinking of a straight Roman one. Have you seen any elephants yet? If you can remember it I would like you to bring me back a small ivory one. If you were an elephant and I asked you to bring me back a small ivory man you would never forget!! What are cheroots like by the way? They sound more like vegetables than cigars. If you can't get an elephant then a small temple bell would be nice.

There is just Mummy and me here now because Uncle Jim is in the Army. It's been very bad with the raids, Jerry coming over night after night. I'm writing this under the stairs in a deckchair and Mummy is dozing next to me. The siren has just gone but it's still quiet. We stay here rather than use the Andersen in the garden, which we both hate. The technical school over the way was bombed last week. Six o'clock in the morning when we thought it was all over and Mummy and me had just got upstairs to bed. We clung to each other whilst these awful whistlings came down and I prayed and prayed. I have never been so frightened. The guns are going now and they sound like dogs, woof, woof, but mostly the planes drop their bombs closer to London.

Mummy was in hospital as I think you know but is out now and has to rest. She looks very well though, much plumper and quite rosy-cheeked. She had to give up smoking, and has started drinking again but there is a terrible shortage!

This seems to be a quiet night for a change but it is early yet. By the time I get to school it often starts again so we have to stay in the shelter, a deep one. Sister Teresa reads the Passion while the guns and things thump and the sweat pours down her face — all in candlelight!

I am sending you a copy of the last picture Uncle Jim took. I'm in the garden with Mummy and Mr Quick the butcher and the little dog with the stumpy tail is called General Slim so that should please you! Mummy and I send our love. God bless you Dad and write soon please,

Helen

Bromley, February 1943

My dear Jim,

This is a hard one so take a hold on yourself. Knowing you I think you probably guessed that Mummy was more ill than we let on. Actually she was dying these past four months Jim and last night she went in her sleep here in your bed. Old Quick and his wife Judy were here with me so that was something. He's been marvellous to both of us and is taking care of all the arrangements. She is to be buried in Bromley cemetery this Saturday in the plot you bought. Quick showed me your letter telling him to help out on anything while you are away so I know everything is all right.

Mummy loved you deeply, Jim, and so do I and I am still here so all is not lost. Just try not to grieve too much. I am staying with Quick and Judy and Slim until things are sorted out. I feel safe with them and that's all that matters. I know you will come through, Jim, and remember I prize you.

My deepest love, Helen

Burgess Hill, June 1944

Dear Jim,

As you see I am in Sussex to get away from the buzz bombs. It was Quick's idea and I am very happy to be in the country at last. We still hear the clatter of those things overhead but they're aimed at poor old London. I'll never forget their sound like a loud tinny kind of back-firing buzz — and then that deep silence when its engine cut and you held your breath wondering if it was your last. Sometimes they explode round here but only in fields.

The family I am with are a cut above the people I'm used to. It's a house and small farm belonging to a Captain Reed, a merchant navy man who got the OBE last year for convoy work. Mrs Reed spends all her time collecting pig food in a little trailer attached to her car, a Standard 8 with a little Union Jack emblem on the nose of the bonnet. There is one son, Daniel, at Brighton College and another, a scientist in London, called Michael. There is a grand piano and Daniel plays Beethoven and we go for long walks over the fields. He knows a lot like you and is going in the navy like his father. He is very attracted to me but very shy because he knows nothing about girls. He has jug ears and is tall and bony like his mother, with the same watery blue eyes and the sort of fresh skin the bones show through in cold weather. He copies animal pictures from the National Geographical magazine, all in oil paint. I've done some too!

Mrs Reed has taken me into Brighton a couple of times on her special allowance petrol (because of the pig food) and I liked it very much, a very pretty town with lots of wormy streets full of little shops that smell like Daniel's room, a sort of outdoors-indoors smell of fishing lines, feathers, glue, bones and birds' eggs. You can't get onto the beach because of the barbed wire and mines and things and the two piers are blown in half but I fell in love with everything .

Last week an artist friend of Michael's came to stay for the weekend with a young Wren officer — Mrs Reed didn't approve! Daniel couldn't take his eyes off her but she was quite plain I thought though very fond of men obviously. I am making some pen and ink studies of flowers and the one enclosed is a forget-me-not as if you didn't know!

Love and fond wishes, Helen

Brighton, October 1947

My Dear Tom and Judy,

It was so good to hear from you and to learn that old Slim is still alive — he'll outlive us all yet. Jim forwarded the letter here where I'm studying at the art school.

I hope you are happy in your new home. What made you retire to Scotland? It never did much for me or my father. Did Jim tell you the poor man was a Jap prisoner of war? Came home fat and pinky-looking and died of cancer. His girl friend had left him and he was too proud to tell us anything. Poor old Dad, he never had much luck.

Jim is an angel and I don't know what I'd do without him. He understands me, knows my strengths and weaknesses, gives me encouragement and God knows we all need that. I will try not to let the side down but, more important, I will try not to let myself down. I hope to go on from here to the Royal College of Art but there's plenty of time.

I don't know what I am going to do with my life except be an artist and enjoy it as much as possible. I sometimes think without Jim nothing would be possible. Thank you both for introducing me to Sussex and give Slim a bone for me!

Affectionately yours, Helen

Brighton, November 1947

Dear Timmy,

I am surprised at your wayward choice of influences (or perhaps I'm not) — but Beardsley indeed! Too sick and commercial for my taste and you go on about his line as if you haven't seen one by Matisse. Perhaps you haven't! George Grosz is sick too but I can accept him because he knows all about rumpled beds and hangovers and people falling to pieces.

Since you ask for a list I'll mention just a few I like: — Piero della Francesca, for his quiet serenity, Van Gogh for his demon, Picasso because he's a cauldron for every idea in art, Manet for his Olympia (I'm surprised you missed this sexy lady), Monet for his mauves and lilies and soft water touch . . . Seurat for *The Bathers* in all its sunlit Sunday afternoon solemnity, Sickert because he's lovely and English, Pissaro for his snow . . . Rembrandt of course — with your eye for women have you noticed the extra arm of the girl in The Great Bed? Then Vermeer I suppose for his balance and harmony. And Matisse and Munch — but I can't go on. Oh, Constable of course, the only one who could look the day in the eye and put it down in a flash. Old Turner I've left out too but no more. You're very lucky being in town within reach of all the galleries. I'll say this much, though, at least you have the nous to spend some weekends in our Regency fairytale! — Next thing, you'll be telling me *I'm* the attraction!

Write soon, Helen

Brighton, January 1948

Dear Timmy,

You had no right to dump me like that with all your artistic friends. I'm really only a provincial you know and pubs and parties are all new to me. I suppose that's why I got drunk although I can't say I enjoyed it very much.

That poet — Omar was it? Definitely 'queer' as you say but very nice and gentle. He took care of me after you disappeared with Sarah what's-her-name. Are you sure she's at the Slade? She hadn't even heard of Professor Tonks. Omar had some marijuana but I didn't try any. I must say you lead a very decadent life in London and God only knows what my guardian would say if he knew how you were trying to corrupt me.

The two Roberts were nice. They studied at Glasgow but it was no Glasgow my Dad would have known. They exhibit at the Lefevre gallery and are really quite famous. McBride, the little one, told me he made his own trousers. There was another painter who interested me, Bacon I believe, rather alone-looking and all in black standing back against the wall in the Black Horse. Think I saw something of his, rather eerie, but I'm very out of touch. Tambi was nice too although I haven't seen his magazine. Who was Tony? I mean, Tony *who?* Find out if you can, he was very interesting and very pretty.

Just to clear the cobwebs away I have been tramping the wintry flanks of the Downs. Descended at Ditchling with wet feet through the rain and after drinks (ginger beer) at the pub felt cleansed and whole again. Needless to say I was not alone.

You were right about Black Rock. Definitely the most unsafe place for a young woman of my stamp: 'Most wild-looking and terribly beautiful' Jack Salmon (stutter and all) thinks I am! Anyway for the third time running a shifty individual tried to pick me up so I'm giving the place a wide berth.

Jim (my guardian) wants to take me to the Tate next weekend so I could be in town Friday if you have any bright ideas. Have you seen *Bicycle Thieves* yet? Jack's been raving about it which is the only thing that puts me off because you know how childlike he is about the undertrodden. I'm interested in what the wops are up to because Jim was there during the war and saw them torn apart. Incidentally, thanks for having faith in me. If I don't get that scholarship I'll be a very sad girl.

> See you on the barricades,
> Love Helen

Brighton, February 1948

Dear Tony,

You write a wicked letter. Thank you. Timmy had no right to tell you what I said but in any case 'pretty' is a special word of mine as he very well knows. It doesn't mean pretty-pretty or effeminate or anything like that. It has a very complimentary meaning private to me so you got it all wrong which is something, I suspect, you don't do very often.

First of all, yes, I would like to meet you again but at the moment I'm working very hard in the hope that I'll get a scholarship to the Royal College — of Art, that is.

Second, the kind of circles Timmy moves in don't move me at all. Not much anyway. Or not at the moment anyway. I may look as if I fit in but really I'm very different, rather shy, studious if you like, and determined not to let the side down — the side being the faith my guardian has in me and which I hope I have in myself.

If there was a 'third' I've forgotten. All I want to say is this: if we become friends it must be in a conventional sort of way, nothing too wild or bohemian if you know what I mean. I'm fairly inexperienced as must be painfully obvious and at the party I was putting on an act because my true self is really rather boring. This is enough about me and probably enough to put you off for a lifetime I shouldn't wonder!

> Yours somewhat wonderingly, Helen.

P.S. I have absolutely no connections with the rather posh Frasers you talk about. My father started a somewhat confused life as a compositor on the Glasgow Evening Herald.

Chelsea, March 1948

Your bed — Monday

Darling Tony,

I will forever cherish this weekend and wonder if you know what you have done for me? I feel as if I have inherited the earth. I want to open the windows and bless the world and tell all the sad people that they must involve themselves in love or die. I want to write you letters like this every day of my life and leave them in little unsuspecting places where you will find them when I am hidden and can watch your face my sweet one. I want to be your girl and live with you through all the days of love and striving and sharing. I want to explore the hours in laughter and calm silence. I want always to hear the tones given off by your heart when you are with me.

I love you, Helen.

Brighton, March 1948

Dearest Jim,

I am sorry if Tony upsets you. He's not the easiest person, I know, but that's Tony and that's the man I love. I don't want to say much more at the moment because everything is new and I haven't come to terms with it — if I ever do. I may be impressionable and naive and all that but it's my life and I have to live it for myself where this precious element called love is concerned. It all sounds so trite and banal and really doesn't bear analysing. How do you analyse a flower which blooms?

Whether I live with Tony down here or not is a bit in the air at the moment. We hate being apart and will have to do something but I won't do anything silly.

Do try, instead of worrying about me, to be *glad* for me.

Love and affection, Helen.

Brighton, April 1948

Dear silly Jim,

Please try and look at the credit side. I am young and fit and talented. I have found a very gentle man just as you are gentle and, all right, so he's a bit of a rebel but then so am I and so are most of the students who are any good. Incidentally you are quite wrong about Tony and National Service. He's not a pacifist although pacifism is the only stand in this world. As it happens he had rheumatic fever as a child and was exempted on medical grounds, otherwise he would have been in and out by now (or dead) because, as you know, he's five years older than me.

But why all these side issues? I know, dear Jim, that you have my best interests at heart and it grieves me that you don't think Tony is good enough for me. I can see that and yet I can't see it. I'm prejudiced. I feel heady with magic. I want it to go on and on, and if it stops, I want to be able to feel thankful that I staked everything for everything rather than staking nothing for nothing.

I *know* I'll get the scholarship. I *know* I'll be happy. I *know* you'll come round to my way of thinking after you see my actions rather than mulling over mere words. Try and have faith, Jim. I'll always love you and never forget what you have done for me even if it doesn't look like it at the moment.

                    With a big kiss, Helen

St John's Wood, April 1948

Dear Tom and Judy,

Thank you for your letter. I feel unbearably low about Jim's death. What makes it so heartbreaking is that it happened because of me. If I hadn't told him about Tony he wouldn't have driven down to Brighton in a rage and there wouldn't have been the accident. And then not to regain consciousness, that was the hardest blow of all, and you're holding on, waiting for the miracle, pretending the brain is still there, and it's all useless, and all you get from the hospital is a load of black magic that makes you want to scream. Oh, God, it's nobody's fault but mine.

I'm staying with a girl friend for a bit but I'm poor company. Tony doesn't understand how I feel about Jim's death — how could he? It was a very special relationship and just as I think Jim was jealous of him, so was he jealous of Jim. One very hurtful thing he said was that I was now free — as if I'd been *tied* to Jim. I never was except by a mutual bond of tenderness. He's left everything to me, by the way, and I don't want a thing. I just want Jim but Jim is scattered to the four winds which was his request and typical of him.

I'm sorry about the funeral, I should have let you know, I should have done lots of things but you must forgive me. You're so kind to ask me to come and stay but somehow I've got to get myself together here amongst the debris. Your letter did help. You two and Slim are the only survivors from the old days and that gives me some comfort. God bless for now,

                    All my love, Helen

St John's Wood, May 1948

Dear Timmy,

I'm staying with Susan Fuller who's keeping an eye on me. I suppose you heard about my guardian's death? Tony will have told you I'm sure. It was a terrible blow and I didn't think I'd survive but Susan stuck with me and the solicitor, Wilkes-Colne, who was Jim's friend. God knows where Tony was. He told me he didn't like death, didn't like to be involved with it and that it was the business of life to stick with life. We had a row but my heart wasn't in it and there is so much to do when someone dies, each act rubbing salt into the wound. On the dark day itself I took a leaf out of your book and swilled down some purple hearts with neat vodka and sailed through, the brave little woman, right to the bitter end when the coffin disappeared behind the curtain. I never want another experience like that.

All this sad business aside, I want to know if you have seen Tony and if you have any idea of what his inexplicable absence is doing to me? I don't want to involve you but since I know you and Tony have become friends you *are* involved willy-nilly. When you see him — look, Tim, it's urgent that I talk to Tony as soon as possible so see what you can do.

Yours as ever, Helen.

St John's Wood, May 1948

Dear Timmy,

I don't understand human beings any more! Sweet God, you meet someone and admit love and they do *this! When* did he go to France? Before or after the funeral? And what is this 'old Transition crowd' you talk about? What's so special about St. Germain des Pres anyway? Soho's always been good enough for him in the past. Anyway I have written to Brice whom I've met a few times, the one who worked with Dylan Thomas, and perhaps he can throw some light.

Love, Helen

Brighton, May 1948

Dear Brice,

Lovely to hear from you and I'm glad you didn't mind me writing care of the pub. It was sweet of you to make enquiries and I'll try the hotel you mention.

I do remember meeting Barker who had a quick, soft voice not unlike Coward's. The other George, Reavey, I also recall, Gascoyne I wouldn't know anyway, not if he's in Paris, and the others mean nothing apart from Nina, Modigliani's old girlfriend, whom I'll never forget. I'm afraid I'm not really up on the literary scene since all my time has been poured into the business of art but I'll try and make up for it one day. I'm living on my nerves at the moment which is a poor substitute for the whisky we drank when we last met.

You mention Johnny Minton and of course I admire his work and remember him very well, slim, vital, with quick warm eyes. I seem to recall leaving you with your friend Julian in the Wheatsheaf was it? And there was that pretty girl Frances. Everything is a bit hazy. What

finished me off was that horsemeat kebab although that's a peccadillo
to what's trying to finish me off at the moment. Thank you again, dear
Brice, you have no idea how your letter cheered me up.

With all best wishes,
Love, Helen

Brighton, May 1948

Tony,

   I can see clearly how the form of this letter could follow the outline
of all the millions which have preceded it through the ages. But I am
not going to pursue that form. Neither do I feel I have any kind of
trump card by telling you I am pregnant. I find it all unutterably
shabby that moments of great beauty must be shaken down to dross
and ugliness and searing waste. No one will love you as I have loved
you. Today, looking at the gulls turning in the wind off the sea, that
love died. There was a sort of twist, a lurch of the bird's wing, and I felt
a splinter of ice stab and melt and it was all over with a sense of
certainty that wasn't even an ache, rather a non-void.

   The money I lent you you can spend on Paris whores which I believe
are to be found behind the Rex cinema. They, my dear Tony, are your
meat. I never want to hear of you or the Hotel pas de Calais again.

Helen.

Westbourne Grove, June 1948

Dear George,

   I want to thank you again for springing me from the hospital. I had
the strength (I think) to get out but not the will. That first time you
came — did you know it was a ward full of aborted women victims?
Naturally everyone thought you were the bastard responsible when
you walked in with the flowers and fruit. You are such a sweet innocent
I didn't have the heart to level with you. O George, if only it had been
your kid! I'm sorry, that's a stupid thing to say. I only mean the chain
of events would have been different.

   The psychiatrist I saw (a Chinese) was worse than useless. He
wanted to know whether I slept with many men. It sounded like:
'dooyar slip wip mini min?' When he turned me down I was ready to
try anything and being me I did. I was lucky to live, put it that way,
but at least it's one unwanted baby less in the world.

   If I sound hard it's because all that soft area in me which makes me
a woman, that part you gamble with when you split your soul with
another human being, has been ripped and bruised by people and
circumstances until I wonder if I'll ever have natural instincts again.

   If only one could go off somewhere and live completely the life
you want to, somewhere with space in which to grow and nurture all
the possibilities and potentialities in oneself. At the moment I wonder

if I'll ever regain my trust to fully love again, to give without wanting to gain. I suppose I must give it time. I must work and get my scholarship. I must stop trying to embrace and reweigh all values, true and false, because all I'm doing is creating the chaos that links the long chain around the centrifugal point of my own identity. I think I would like to feel an absolute freedom to live, love and work uninhibited and unconditionally!

There! Now I've probably frightened you and I don't want that. I want your friendship and the understanding you're so good at. I've learnt much in the past few months, enough to know that friends like you don't grow on trees as my mother used to say.

O how I go on! Give me a ring, George, when you're in town. I miss the old Brighton days and want all the news.

Love, then, Helen

Chelsea, August 1950

O George I'm so sorry I was drunk after all the trouble you took to create a special evening for us. Since I quit the College I've been miserable and low. Although I jibed at everything I at least had a daily pattern to hide in and shut out some of the clamour that passes for reality when you go naked through the days.

There is one thing I must point out to you before it is too late. *Please* do not fall in love with me. I am wild and capricious with an exaggerated sense of my own freedom to do what I like with my own life. Meanwhile more often than not I sit in this studio and feel I'm on a stricken vessel, so like a prolonged sea-sickness is the feeling inside me. That's probably why I'm drinking too much and lately there have been other things too depressing to go into.

What you need George is a really nice strong woman. I do not, correspondingly, need a nice strong man. I don't feel I need anyone because there's too much pain involved. The world outside these windows is full of dumb furies that I can do without.

This is very melancholy stuff and I'm sure it's the drugs talking, all the poisons I've been accumulating in my system, so I'll say goodnight, sweet George, and see you who knows when?

Lots of love, Helen

Branscombe Lodge, April 1953

Dear Ralph,

I've been building up to this place for the last three years and you must have guessed something like that when you brought me here. I hate the place because herds of anything depress me, particularly when they're fellow victims sprawled out glassy-eyed under bell jars of private misery.

I suppose you noticed the place is set in what can only be a

petrified forest since it's April (isn't it?) and I see no unbuddings, not
the stirring of a green fuse. Waiting for spring I keep thinking of
Botticelli's *Primavera*. The model for that painting was called
Simonetta Vespucci and I had a lover once who, shortly before he
changed into a plebian bastard, told me I resembled her. True or false
Ralph?

The head shrink here is dour, humourless and possessed of that
innate superiority of one who walks tall among the fallen. It's very
wrong that individuals like him can be the arbiters of suffering for
which they feel contempt and of which they have no experience.
We're the fodder for academical and scientific papers and for the
corrupt mathematics of advancement.

Will you please not try to phone Ralph — there is only one phone
theatrically unprivate and crowded by desperadoes as if it were the last
link with the planet Earth.

I will only add that the head shrink has pretensions to digging at
pregenital disturbances via the drug LSD — a very dangerous toy. Well,
he will get no Freudian mouse droppings from me thank you very
much. There is nothing wrong with me which fulfilment as a woman,
first, and as an artist, second, wouldn't have put right. I don't know.
Meanwhile, you saved my life probably although I'm in two minds
about that mystery.

There is no one less rewarding, Ralph, than an embittered woman.
I tried so hard not to let the drip drip of acrimony into my heart
and for a time there I was winning, or so I thought, until suddenly
I was in a shipwreck.

> Thank you dear Ralph, Helen

Battersea, June 1955

Dear Mr Wilkes-Colne,

If the only means of raising money is to sell the Bromley house
(since it's empty) then please go ahead and sell it. It's nothing but a
millstone of memories anyway and I need the money. Do not be canny
but just SELL or it will be too late. In the meantime I would like you,
on the strength of the proposed sale, to arrange with my bank for
another overdraft or loan or whatever. I am not well and desperately
need to get away from everything.

> Yours sincerely, Helen Fraser

Colvend, January 1956

My dear you did it! O George your successful exhibition is great
news. I'm so happy for you and so unhappy for myself — but then I
have only myself to blame. There was a time when I had it all but I
let it slip through my fingers. Now I don't care about me but only
about lovely people like you. The fact that one of our little band won

through is enough. I shall toast your success with my last bottle of champagne.

I am working here after a fashion. Painting the sea. Engrossed with waves. Caught up with the big wintry wash of the Solway estuary. In the little niche which I inhabit close to the edge of the sea I am one with the creatures who land up high and dry between the tides. In some of them the little clock of life keeps time and the next tide renews them. For others the tide is too late and they join the rest of the flotsam.

I love the elemental loneliness here with just gulls and curlews and oystercatchers for company. The geese are arriving for their winter banquet on the salt marsh and there is a coming together and a going away with me caught up in no-woman's-land.

Thinking of how it was once I see clearly, now, that there is a moment which you don't plan for but which, when it comes, you find yourself rich enough in love and optimism to accommodate fiercely. If you're lucky you maybe go on to build homes for heroes and art and all the rest. Oh, George. *You* know that I had such a moment and in the aftermath, when perhaps nothing is so perfect, I fell back on a hard pride and destroyed in one decision everything that was the future in me. I would not pluck from the flames and so instead lived to see the ashes. However, there is a larger canvas and all the figures on it are transient. There are no figures on the canvas before me. Just one big wave into which I think I want to sink and be washed ever so gently away from my sins, away from the taste of wormwood in my mouth. Do I sound defeatist? I don't mean to. I don't care any more anyway. I mean if it's not a wave it's something else isn't it? And there are worse ways to leave the departure point. With a wave you can at least wish someone bon voyage if it comes to it. And if it comes to it will you do that George? Wish me bon voyage and think of me sometimes when you watch the sea, which you love, and if you hear a siren call — you never know . . . it might be me. Shall we dance?

Helen.

THE DOG IT WAS THAT DIED

by Tom Stoppard

For Richard Imison

Tom Stoppard has written for radio, television and the stage. His work for radio includes *The Dissolution of Dominic Boot* (1964); *M is for Moon Among Other Things* (1964); *If You're Glad I'll Be Frank* (1966); *A Separate Peace* (1966); *Albert's Bridge* (1967) and *Where Are They Now?* (1976). For television he has written *A Walk On Water* (1963; later rewritten for the stage as *Enter a Free Man*, 1968); *Teeth* (1967); *Another Moon Called Earth* (1967; the seed of *Jumpers*); *Neutral Ground* (1968); *Artist Descending a Staircase* (1972); *Three Men in a Boat* (1975); *The Boundary* (1975 with Clive Exton); and *Professional Foul* (1977). His stage plays include *The Gamblers* (1965); *Rosencrantz and Guildenstern Are Dead* (1966); *Tango* (1966; an adaptation of Mrozek's play); *The Real Inspector Hound* (1968); *After Magritte* (1970); *Jumpers* (1972); *The House of Bernardo Alba* (1973; adapted from Lorca's play); *Travesties* (1974); *Dirty Linen* (1976); *Every Good Boy Deserves Favour* (1977); *Night and Day* (1978); *Dogg's Hamlet, Cahoot's Macbeth* (1979); *Undiscovered Country* (1979; a version of Schnitzler's *Das Weite Land*); *On the Razzle* (1981; an adaptation of Nestroy's *Einen Jux will er sich machen*) and *The Real Thing* (1982).

The Dog It Was That Died was first broadcast on BBC Radio 3 on 9th December 1982. The cast was as follows:

PURVIS	Dinsdale Landen
BLAIR	Charles Gray
HOGBEN	Kenneth Cranham
SLACK	Peter Tuddenham
PAMELA	Penelope Keith
MRS RYAN	Katherine Parr
ARLON	Stephen Murray
MATRON	Betty Marsden
SEDDON	John Le Mesurier
VICAR	Noel Howlett
CHIEF	Maurice Denham
WREN	Lockwood West

Director John Tydeman

Scene One

London at night. The sound of PURVIS's *footsteps on the pavement. An occasional vehicle passing, not very close.* PURVIS *is coming up to retirement age. As he walks he is singing quietly, disjointedly, cheerfully . . . songs of farewell: the one beginning 'Goodbye-ee . . .' and 'Goodbye Piccadilly . . .' . . . and 'We don't want to leave you but . . .'*

Over this is PURVIS's *voice reading through a letter he has written. The singing voice and the footsteps, together with the occasional road and river traffic, continue intermittently underneath.*

PURVIS (*in voice-over, reading letter*). Dear Blair. I have decided I have had enough of this game and I'm getting out but before I take the plunge . . . (*He chuckles briefly but pulls himself together*) . . . before I take the plunge I thought I'd give you a tip which if you handle it right could put you in the top spot in the Department, assuming that that is what you want. Not that I have any fastidious scruples myself about the Chief having an opium den in his house in Eaton Square — perhaps that is something more of us should be doing — but I dare say the Prime Minister would take a different view. That was the tip, by the way. I wish I had something more on him to give you but gone are the days when a man could be brought down by being named in the divorce courts, even for sexual misconduct with the wife of a subordinate, and I only mention it now because your good lady (is she called Pamela? — I only met her once) may have been pulling the wool over your eyes and you have always been more than decent to me. So you will have to do what you can with the opium den, and my only regret is that I won't be here to enjoy the brouhaha . . .

The here-and-now PURVIS *adds a few ha-ha's.*

Actually, it's not my *only* regret because I was looking forward to taking a belly dancer to Buckingham Palace — if the invitation was anything to do with you, many thanks for the thought. She's a splendid girl, and would have made a bit of a splash. But now it's left to me to do that. Thanks, anyway. There's something of mine which has been in the family for ages and as I'm the last of the line you may like to have it. It's supposed to have belonged to a one-legged sea captain who inspired the character of Long John Silver and I thought you might find a place for it in your folly. In all honesty, I saw one just like it on a piano in Cork Castle or somewhere, which gives one pause for thought, but I'll send it round anyway.

PURVIS *is now walking across Chelsea Bridge and Big Ben is heard distantly striking the quarter hour.*

Well, I think that's about all. I hope I won't be bobbing up again so there shouldn't be any problem with the remains. I have left enough in the kitty for a plaque on the wall of St Luke's where I am church warden, and I would be grateful if you could make sure this is done. The vicar bears a grudge against me but if he starts making trouble you can take it from me that on the subject of that savoury business the choir is lying its head off man and boy, especially Hoskins, third from the end with the eyelashes. An enquiry would clear my name but I have no wish to see the diocese dragged through the mud. That is a fate I have reserved for — yours ever, Rupert Purvis.

(*Now speaking 'live'*). Well, this seems to be about the middle of the bridge . . . if I can manage the parapet . . . (*He grunts and heaves himself up.*) I'm too old for this game . . . nice breeze on the river anyway . . . quiet as the grave and black as your hat — to hell with the lot of them, oh dear me . . . (*He starts to sniffle, all cheerfulness gone.*) Never mind, it's all over now. Off I . . . go . . .

The last word is extended with PURVIS's *plunge, which ends unexpectedly with the sound of a quite large dog in sudden and short-lived pain.*

Scene Two

St. James's Park in the daytime. Big Ben is striking Ten. BLAIR *is middle-aged and a gentleman.* HOGBEN *is young and perhaps less of a gentleman.*

BLAIR. Good morning. On the dot.

HOGBEN. I see the tulips are in glorious bloom.

BLAIR. Absolutely. What can I do for you, Hogben?

HOGBEN. I'm sorry — do we know each other?

BLAIR. I prefer thingummies myself. What's all this about?

HOGBEN. I see the tulips are in glorious bloom.

BLAIR. So you said. I prefer hollyhocks myself. (*Pause.*) Hibiscus?
(*Pause.*) Come on, Hogben. I'm Blair. We've met. A couple of years
ago up in Blackheath, don't you remember?

HOGBEN. I'm afraid not.

BLAIR. Two days and nights in the back of a laundry van watching
a dead-letter drop for a pigeon who never turned up . . . I'll never
forget Blackheath.

HOGBEN (*carefully*). I *was* in Blackheath once.

BLAIR. Of course you were. That was you in the white apron, brought
me chicken in a basket. I mean a laundry basket. So stop fooling
about. (*Pause.*) Gladioli? (*Pause.*) All right, I'll just sit on this bench
and enjoy the view. The view north from St James's Park is
utterly astonishing, I always think. Domes and cupolas, strange
pinnacles and spires. A distant prospect of St Petersburg, one
imagines . . . Where does it all go to when one is in the middle of it,
standing in Trafalgar Square with Englishness on every side?
Monumental Albion, giving credit where credit is due to some
sketchbook of a Grand Tour, but all as English as a 49 bus.

HOGBEN. With or without chips?

BLAIR. As I remember it was a baked potato in silver foil, and a
Kit Kat.

HOGBEN. Hydrangeas.

BLAIR. That was it. I prefer hydrangeas myself.

HOGBEN. I'm sorry, sir, but . . .

BLAIR. Perfectly all right. Keen gardener are you?

HOGBEN. Do you run a man called Purvis, Mr Blair?

BLAIR. Rupert Purvis?

HOGBEN. Yes. He tried to kill himself last night. He killed a dog
instead.

BLAIR. I see.

HOGBEN. Sir?

BLAIR. I said — I see.

HOGBEN. Oh. Well. Well, he jumped off Chelsea Bridge at three
sixteen this morning, precisely at high tide. A precise man,
Mr Purvis.

BLAIR. Yes.

HOGBEN. Unfortunately he landed on a barge.

BLAIR. You mean fortunately.

HOGBEN. I was looking at it from his point of view.

BLAIR. Of course.

HOGBEN. In fact he landed on a barge dog. The dog broke Purvis's fall. Purvis broke the dog's back. The barge dropped Purvis off down-stream at St. Thomas's Hospital.

BLAIR. And that's where he is now?

HOGBEN. Yes, sir.

BLAIR. Well, I'll pop along and see him. Thank you, Hogben.

HOGBEN. There is something else, sir.

BLAIR. Yes. What kind of dog was it?

HOGBEN. I don't know, sir.

BLAIR. Well, it wouldn't be anything special. Fifty pounds, more than ample, wouldn't you say?

HOGBEN. I hadn't really thought, sir.

BLAIR. I would say fifty. If your Chief won't wear it, I dare say mine will.

HOGBEN. I didn't want to mention this to your Chief.

BLAIR. Oh, he's all right for fifty, don't worry. You worry too much, Hogben, if I may say so. I'm grateful to you for taking this trouble but it would have been quite all right for you to come to the office.

HOGBEN. No, sir. I thought it was better to talk outside. It's not about the dog, sir. It's about a letter. Purvis posted a letter a few minutes before he jumped. We retrieved it.

BLAIR. You've been following him, Hogben.

HOGBEN. We didn't know he was one of our own.

BLAIR. He wasn't yours, he was mine. Still is.

HOGBEN. That's what I meant.

BLAIR. Well, who did you think he was?

HOGBEN. We thought he was one of theirs.

BLAIR. I see.

HOGBEN. He was followed from Highgate Hill to a house in Church Street, Chelsea.

BLAIR. He lives there.

HOGBEN. Yes, so I gather. He left the house again just before three, leaving all the lights on. He knew he wouldn't have to pay any more bills. He walked to the river.

BLAIR. Posting a letter on the way. Whereabouts in Highgate did you follow him from? Highgate Hill Square?

HOGBEN. You obviously know all about it.

BLAIR. Everybody knows their safe house. Red Square we call it.

HOGBEN. We call it Dunkremlin.

BLAIR. Why?

HOGBEN. Sir?

BLAIR. Why did you follow him? Was he acting suspiciously?

HOGBEN. Not exactly suspiciously. He walked out of the front door, slamming it behind him.

BLAIR. Well, I give him a pretty free rein. When did you realise he was Q6?

HOGBEN. It was the letter. Here you are, sir. You understand, sir, that we had to open all the letters in the box in order to ascertain . . .

BLAIR. Yes, of course. Thank you. I'll read it later. Anything else?

HOGBEN. Sir?

BLAIR. I said — anything else?

HOGBEN. Well, the letter's a bit . . . Would you say that Mr Purvis had been overworking lately?

BLAIR. Well, *I* haven't been overworking him. But of course I can't speak for *them*.

Scene Three

A hospital ward.

BLAIR. Well, Purvis, this is all very silly. What on earth did you think you were doing jumping off bridges?

PURVIS. Oh, hello, sir. How good of you to come.

BLAIR. Not at all. Are you quite comfortable?

PURVIS. Yes, thank you. I'm grateful for the private room.

BLAIR. I meant with your feet winched up like that. You put me in mind of a saucy postcard.

PURVIS. I put the nurses in mind of midwifery. But I appreciate your not mincing words. You're the first person who has mentioned the word jump or bridge since I got here. I thought I must have imagined it all. By the way, was there something about a dog?

BLAIR. Yes. You're the first person to jump off a bridge onto a dog. The reverse one often used to see at the Saturday morning cinema, of course.

PURVIS. Men jumping off dogs onto . . . ?

BLAIR. No, dogs jumping off bridges onto . . .

PURVIS. Oh yes. What a relief anyway. I was beginning to think I'd gone cuckoo.

BLAIR. Your relief may be premature. There's nothing cuckoo about imagining things. Cuckoo is jumping off bridges. Are you in any sort of trouble?

PURVIS. Well, one had a bit of a crise, you know.

BLAIR. Yes. Do you remember writing me a letter?

PURVIS. Have you received it already?

BLAIR. Special delivery.

PURVIS. I wasn't going to mention it.

BLAIR. I shouldn't have done so.

PURVIS. A bit of a shaker, I expect.

BLAIR. Well, these things happen in all families.

PURVIS. You mean that business about your wife. I'm sorry. It's the last thing one would have expected of a woman who runs a donkey sanctuary — concubine to an opium addict.

BLAIR (*huffily*). Now look here, Purvis —

PURVIS. Yes, I'm so sorry — one loses all one's social graces when one expected to be dead.

BLAIR. I didn't mean *my* family. I meant Q6. People having what you call a bit of a *crise*. I suggest we draw the veil, eh? Least said soonest mended.

PURVIS. You must do as you think fit. Personally I think you'd make an excellent number one, but I can quite see that you might take the view that it's nobody's business what the Chief gets up to in his own time so long as he doesn't bring his pipe to the office. Perhaps you think I'm a bit of a cad for sneaking?

BLAIR. These decisions are never easy. By the way, where did this story come from?

PURVIS. It's all over Highgate.

BLAIR. I see.

PURVIS. I was up there last night actually.

BLAIR. Really?

PURVIS. I went to visit my friend.

BLAIR. Oh yes?

PURVIS. He was none too pleased.

BLAIR. No?

PURVIS. I was after some information.

BLAIR. And did you get it?

PURVIS. No. I said to him, look, I said, can you just remind me —
what is the essential thing we're supposed to be in it for? — the
ideological nub of the matter? Is it power to the workers: is it the
means of production, distribution and exchange: is it each
according to his needs: is it the expropriation of the expropriators?
Know what he said? Historical inevitability! You're joking, I said.
Pull the other one, it's got bells on. No, you'll have to do better
than that. Something can't be good just because it's *inevitable*. It
may be good and it may be inevitable, but that's no *reason,* it may
be *rotten* and inevitable. He couldn't see it. So I left. None the
wiser. Perhaps you could help me on this one, Blair.

BLAIR. Oh . . . I don't know . . . they did give us a run-down on it
years ago . . . I didn't take much notice. There was something
called the value of labour capital which seemed to be important but
I never understood what it was.

PURVIS. No, I mean from your side of the fence.

BLAIR. Mine?

PURVIS. Yes. It's important to me. Can you remind me, what was the
gist of it? — the moral and intellectual foundation of Western
society in a nutshell.

BLAIR. I'm sorry, my mind's gone blank.

PURVIS. Come on — democracy . . . free elections, free expression,
free market forces . . .

BLAIR. Oh yes, that was it.

PURVIS. Yes, but how did we deal with the argument that all this
freedom merely benefits the people who already have the edge? I
mean, freedom of expression advantages the articulate . . . Do
you see?

BLAIR. You're going a bit fast for me, Purvis. I never really got beyond
us being British and them being atheists and Communists. There's
no arguing with that, is there? Are you quite sure you aren't in
any sort of trouble?

PURVIS. Depends what you mean by trouble.

BLAIR. Your letter mentioned some unsavoury business with choirboys.

PURVIS. *Savoury* business, not unsavoury business.

BLAIR. Savoury business?

PURVIS. Yes. You know what a savoury is. Mushrooms on toast . . . sardines . . . or, in this case, Welsh rarebit.

BLAIR. I see. Well, you just have a jolly good rest, Rupert, take the weight off your feet . . .

PURVIS. As you see . . .

BLAIR. Yes, of course. But we'll soon have you back on them. You were lucky.

PURVIS. Luckier than the dog.

BLAIR. Yes. It was the dog that died.

Scene Four

The garden of BLAIR'*s house.*

BLAIR. I admit it looks odd. The question is does it look odd enough?

SLACK. It looks odd enough to me, sir.

BLAIR. I'm not convinced, Mr Slack. I *do* like the mullioned window between the Doric columns — that has a quality of coy desperation, like a spinster gatecrashing a costume ball in a flowered frock . . . and the pyramid on the portico is sheer dumb insolence. All well and good. I think it's the gothic tower that disappoints. It isn't quite *there*. It's gothic but not gothick with a K. Should we ruin one of the butresses?

SLACK. Ruin it, sir?

BLAIR. Mm . . . Make it a bit of a ruin. Or should we wait for the ivy to catch up?

SLACK. I should wait for the ivy, sir. We're going to have our hands full with the obelisk. Is it all right to lower away?

BLAIR. Yes, lower away.

SLACK (*calls out*). Lower away!

BLAIR. The crane has to swing it over slightly to the right.

SLACK. No, sir, it's centred on top of the tower.

BLAIR. But it's lop-sided.

SLACK. Only from where we're standing.

BLAIR. But surely, Mr Slack, if it's centred on top of the tower it should look centred from everywhere.

SLACK. That would be all right with a round, Norman tower, sir,
but with your octagonal gothic tower the angles of the parapet
throw the middle out.

BLAIR. Throw the middle out — ?

SLACK. The obelisk will look centred from the terrace, sir.

BLAIR. But it has to look centred from my study window as well.

SLACK. Can't be done now — you'd have had to have one side of
the tower squared up with the window.

BLAIR. Hold everything.

SLACK (*shouts*). Hold everything!

BLAIR. This obviously needs the superior intelligence of Mrs B. I'll
go and fetch her from the paddock.

SLACK. She's in the drawing-room, sir.

BLAIR. I thought she was operating on one of the donkeys.

SLACK. That's right, sir.

Scene Five

Indoors: modest donkey noises.

BLAIR (*entering*). Pamela . . .

The donkey brays and kicks the floor.

PAMELA. Hang on, Mrs Ryan.

BLAIR. I say, do be careful of my clocks.

The room is going tick-tock rather a lot.

PAMELA. You've come just at the right moment. Mrs Ryan, you're
doing very well but I can't do the stitches if there's so much
movement.

MRS RYAN. Right ho, dear.

PAMELA. Giles, you hang on to her legs.

BLAIR. I haven't really got time for all this.

PAMELA. Not Mrs Ryan's legs, Giles, Empy's.

BLAIR. Oh.

PAMELA. There, there, Empy. Soon be over.

BLAIR. Look, Pamela, the donkey sanctuary is supposed to be the
paddock. The drawing-room is supposed to be sanctuary *from* the
the donkeys.

PAMELA. This is the only fire lit today and I needed it to sterilise the instrument. Hold her neck, Mrs Ryan.

MRS RYAN. Right ho, dear.

PAMELA. Poor Empy got into a fight with Don Juan. It's only a couple of stitches . . . here we go everybody . . .

Silence, except for the ticking and tocking. Then the donkey brays and kicks.

BLAIR. For God's sake — she nearly kicked over my American Townsend.

PAMELA. Well, hold her *still.*

A tense silence, marked by an orchestra of ticks and tocks.

How long have I got before they all go off?

BLAIR. About a minute.

PAMELA. I don't see why they have to be *going* all the time.

BLAIR. If they weren't going they wouldn't be clocks, they'd be bric-a-brac. The long delay in the invention of the clock was all to do with the hands going round. If the hands didn't have to go round, the Greeks could have had miniature Parthenons on their mantle shelves with clock faces stuck into the pediments permanently showing ten past two or eight thirty-five . . .

MRS RYAN. Were you expecting a clock today, sir? A package came for you, special delivery, sender's name Purvis.

BLAIR. Oh yes. Do you remember Purvis, Pamela?

PAMELA. Don't talk to me while I'm stitching. Isn't Empy being brave? Good girl.

BLAIR. I introduced you to him at the Chief's Christmas drinks. You said there was something funny about him. Pretty sharp. He tried to kill himself the other night. He killed a dog instead. He's sent me a family heirloom. I suppose I'll have to send it back now.

PAMELA. That must be what the note from Security was about. They opened your parcel in transit. They thought it was suspicious.

BLAIR. No, no I know all about it. Purvis has sent me an old sea-captain's wooden peg-leg.

PAMELA. No he hasn't, he's sent you a stuffed parrot.

BLAIR. That's what I meant. There's one just like it on the piano in Cork Castle. That remind's me, there's a serious problem with the obelisk on the tower. It's going to look lop-sided depending on where one is standing, even though it's in the middle.

PAMELA. That's because of the corners. You should have had a round tower.

BLAIR. Why didn't you tell me?

PAMELA. I didn't think it mattered. The whole thing is fairly loopy anyway.

BLAIR. It's the old story — never change anything that works! I had in mind the obelisk at Plumpton Magna where they have a round tower but I thought I would go octagonal. It's entirely my own fault.

PAMELA. You mean your own folly. Can you reach the forceps?

BLAIR. Where are they?

PAMELA. On the grate.

BLAIR. Right.

BLAIR yelps as he drops the forceps. He yelps louder as the donkey kicks him. The donkey brays. All the clocks start to chime and strike. The donkey gallops across the wooden floor and then out of earshot.

BLAIR. She kicked me!

PAMELA. I know just how she felt.

BLAIR. Well, the forceps were red hot.

The clocks are still going strong.

MRS RYAN. Is it all right if I get on now, dear?

PAMELA. Yes, all right, Mrs Ryan. Good job the French windows were open.

MRS RYAN switches on a vacuum cleaner.
PAMELA fades out calling for Empy as she leaves the room.

MRS RYAN. Can you lift your leg, dear?

BLAIR. No, I can't. The knee is swelling visibly.

MRS RYAN. Don't worry, dear. I'll vacuum round you.

The clocks continue to strike.

Scene Six

St James's Park. Big Ben is striking.

BLAIR. Good morning. I see the tulips are fighting fit.

HOGBEN. There's no need for that, sir.

BLAIR. No, no, just a passing remark. I thought you were keen on the things. Anyway, what's up?

HOGBEN. You remember that letter Purvis wrote you?

BLAIR. Yes?

HOGBEN. It's been on my mind.

BLAIR. You really *do* worry too much, Hogben.

HOGBEN. Didn't it worry you, Mr Blair?

BLAIR. Well, some of it of course . . . but every family has occasional problems.

HOGBEN. You mean about Mrs Blair?

BLAIR. No, I don't mean anything of the sort. I really don't understand how some people's minds work. I was talking about Q6. We're a small department with, I like to think, a family feeling, and we have occasional problems, that's all.

HOGBEN. I'm sorry. I didn't believe a word of it, of course. The whole letter was raving mad. I never read anything so obviously off its trolley. That's what worries me about it, as a matter of fact. That's why it's on my mind.

BLAIR. What do you mean, Hogben?

HOGBEN. Well, sir — the opium den in Eaton Square, the belly dancer at Buckingham Palace, the sea captain's piano-leg —

BLAIR. Parrot — it was a stuffed parrot.

HOGBEN. Well, whatever. And some scandal with an entire male voice choir.

BLAIR. I asked Purvis about that. He said it involved a Welsh rarebit.

HOGBEN. You see what I mean.

BLAIR. No.

HOGBEN. I think the letter smells. I think he overdid it. I think he's shamming, Mr Blair.

BLAIR. Shamming what?

HOGBEN. I think Purvis *wanted* you to think he'd gone off his trolley.

BLAIR. But Hogben . . . he did jump off Chelsea Bridge.

HOGBEN. At high tide. The absolute top. To the minute.

BLAIR. Exactly.

HOGBEN. When there was the shortest possible distance to fall.

BLAIR. Everybody goes too fast for me nowadays.

HOGBEN. Think about it, sir. There he is in the Soviet safe house in Highgate. What he's doing there I leave an open question for the minute. He makes a conspicuous departure, practically begging to be followed. He walks all the way home just to make it easy. He comes out flashing a letter which he posts, and then off to the bridge and over he goes — just as a handy barge is there to pick him up.

BLAIR. But he landed *on* the barge.

HOGBEN. It went slightly wrong. Especially for the dog.

BLAIR. You're not serious?

HOGBEN. No, I'm not. It's just not on. Apart from anything else the bargee and his family have been scudding about the river for three generations, real Tories, can't abide foreigners, wouldn't even eat the food. So that one is a non-starter. I'm just showing that the facts would fit more than one set of possibilities. There's something wrong with that letter. I know there is. You wouldn't like to tell me what Purvis was doing up in Highgate?

BLAIR. He was discussing political philosophy.

HOGBEN. I suppose you people know what you're doing.

BLAIR. Well, one tries.

HOGBEN. Where is Purvis now?

BLAIR. Convalescing. We maintain a house on the Norfolk coast, as a rest home for those of our people who . . . need a rest. Sea breezes, simple exercise, plain food, T.V. lounge, own grounds, wash-basins in every room . . . It's like an hotel, one of those appalling English hotels. So I'm told — I've never been there.

HOGBEN. A rest home for people who crack up?

BLAIR. You could put it like that. Or you could say it's a health farm.

HOGBEN. A funny farm?

BLAIR. I think that's about as much as I can help you, Hogben.

HOGBEN. How is Purvis now?

BLAIR. I'm going to go and see him in a day or two. I'll let you know how I find him.

HOGBEN. *If* you find him. Is there a gate to this place?

BLAIR. No, as far as I know Purvis could make a dash for it in his wheelchair any time he chooses.

HOGBEN. I'm sorry if I seem to be obstinate. But there is something funny about that letter, sir. I don't know what it is.

BLAIR. Well, I'm afraid I must be getting back.

HOGBEN. Thank you for coming out to meet me . . . You seem to have been in the wars.

BLAIR. Got kicked on the knee by a donkey, nothing serious.
Goodbye — careful with my hand, burned my fingers . . . Oh, how
I love this view! What a skyline! All the way up Whitehall from
Parliament Square, Trafalgar Square, St James's . . . It's like one
enormous folly.

Scene Seven

*The rest home. Sea sounds and gulls. A motor mower at work in the
background.*
     ARLON is an old buffer who is mowing the lawn not far off.

ARLON. Ahoy there!

BLAIR. Er — good afternoon.

ARLON (*approaching*). Spanking day!

BLAIR. Yes, indeed. Where would I find . . . ?

ARLON. Quite a swell.

BLAIR. Thank you.

ARLON. Force three, south sou-west, running before the wind all
     way down from London, just the ticket.

BLAIR. Where would I find Dr Sed — ?

ARLON. Hang on, let me turn this thing off.

     The engine of the mower is cut to idling speed.

     That's better. Welcome aboard.

BLAIR. I don't want to interrupt your mowing.

ARLON. Glad of the excuse to heave to, been tacking up and down
     all morning.

BLAIR. You're doing an excellent job here.

ARLON. Good of you to say so.

BLAIR. Deeply satisfying, I should think.

ARLON. Well, it's not everybody's idea of fun, running a bin for a
     couple of dozen assorted nervous wrecks and loonies, but I
     suppose it's better than cleaning spitoons in the fo'c'sle — even when
     London won't give us the money to pay a proper gardener. Still,
     there we are — you must be Blair. What happened to your fingers?
     Ice in the rigging?

BLAIR. How do you do? I'm sorry, I didn't realise . . . You are the
     warden here?

ARLON. I prefer the term keeper, just as I prefer the term loony.
     Let's call things by their proper name, eh?

BLAIR. Yes . . . Dr Seddon, isn't it?

ARLON. Commodore.

BLAIR. Commodore Seddon?

ARLON. You've come about Purvis, the scourge of the tidal bestiary, the one-man mission to keep the inland waterways dog-free, correct?

BLAIR. Well, yes.

ARLON. These secret service types, once they crack they can't stop babbling. Are you a member of the Naval and Military Club?

BLAIR. I don't recall.

ARLON. I used to be. But after certain words exchanged between myself and a brother officer in the card room it was not possible for me to remain. I said to the secretary, 'Look, chum,' I said, 'we Arlons have been gentlefolk in Middlesex for five generations. We kept our own carriage when Twickenham was a hamlet and the Greenslades were as dust under our wheels, and I will not be called a jumped up suburban cardsharp by a man whose grandfather bought a baronetcy from the proceeds of an ointment claiming to enlarge the female breast' — a spurious claim moreover as an old shipmate of mine, now unhappily gone to her Maker, might have attested. Her Maker having made her the shape of an upended punt. Wouldn't you have done the same — ?

BLAIR. I . . .

ARLON. I know you would. As far as that nine of hearts was concerned, I accept that salting it away behind one's braces for a rainy day does not fall within the rules of Grand National Whist as the game is understood on land, I accept that without reservation, but certain words were uttered and cannot be unuttered, they are utterly and unutterably uttered, Blair, and if you want to do a chap a favour the next time you find yourself in St James's, I'd like you to take out your service revolver and go straight up to Greenslade and —

BLAIR. Absolutely. Consider it done.

ARLON. Thank you, Blair. I shall sleep easier.

BLAIR. Don't mention it. By the way, do you happen to know where I mght find Dr Seddon?

MATRON (*approaching across the gravel*). Good afternoon!

ARLON. I expect Matron will know. Say nothing about this. Take in a couple of reefs and batten the hatches.

BLAIR. Thank you very much.

MATRON. Mr Blair?

BLAIR. Good afternoon.

MATRON. Thank you, Commodore — please continue with the mowing.

ARLON. I don't take orders from you, you're just a figurehead and I've seen better ones on the sharp end of a dredger.

MATRON. Now, Commodore, do you want your rum ration with your cocoa or don't you?

ARLON. If I mow the lawn it is because it pleases me to do so.

The mowing continues.

MATRON. Welcome to Clifftops, Mr Blair. I saw you talking to the Commodore from the window. He's one of our more difficult guests. I do hope it wasn't too awkward for you.

BLAIR. It's all right. He caught me on the wrong foot for a moment.

MATRON. I noticed the limp. You'll be wanting Dr Seddon. Let's go inside.

BLAIR. Thank you.

They walk a few yards across the gravel and then they are inside.

MATRON. He's probably looking in on the ping pong players in the library.

BLAIR. Ping pong in the library. Isn't that rather disturbing?

MATRON. I suppose it is but most of them are already rather disturbed when they get here. See that one over there? He's *dangerous.* Let me take your coat.

BLAIR. I haven't got a coat.

MATRON. Never mind — (*opening a door*) in here — quick!

BLAIR *is pushed through the door.*

BLAIR. What — ?

MATRON. Sssh.

The door closes.

BLAIR (*whispering*). Where are we?

MATRON. In the coat cupboard. We haven't got long so don't waste a minute.

BLAIR. Really Matron . . .

MATRON. Don't Matron me, I blew your cover the moment you showed your limp. I'm match-fit and ready to go — parachute, midget submarine, you name it. The last show wasn't my fault, the maps were out of date.

BLAIR. Will you please open the —

The door is opened.

SEDDON. Who is in there?

BLAIR. Ah, good afternoon — I'm looking for Doctor Seddon.

MATRON (*sweetly*). And this, of course, is the coat cupboard.

BLAIR. Awfully nice.

SEDDON. Thank you, Bilderbeck. You may leave our visitor to me now.

MATRON. Matron to you, if you don't mind.

SEDDON. Have you had your tablets?

MATRON (*receding*). Mind your own business.

SEDDON. That's Bilderbeck. She used to dress up as a matron to oblige a chap she got mixed up with in Washington. When she was confronted with the photographs she insisted that she was giving him first aid and she's been sticking to her story ever since. It's the only uniform we have here. We found that they tended to set people off. So we're all in civies. Not even a white coat, as you see. You must be Blair. I'm Dr Seddon.

BLAIR. How do you do. Giles Blair. Look, don't take this amiss but would you have any form of identification?

SEDDON. First sensible remark I've heard today, counting the ones by the staff. Let's go to my office and have a cup of tea.

BLAIR. Thanks very much.

SEDDON. This way. How are things in London?

BLAIR. Relatively sane.

SEDDON. I know what you mean. My time with the firm was excellent preparation for Clifftops.

BLAIR. Oh . . . were you — ?

SEDDON. Q10.

BLAIR. Code breaking?

SEDDON. Code making. You may have heard of consonantal transposition. Scramble your own telephone. That was my contribution to the fun and games.

BLAIR. Really? No, I . . .

SEDDON. We go up these stairs now. Yes, they never took it up. Said it was too difficult, or too simple, one or the other.

BLAIR. How did it work?

SEDDON. Rosetransing stantocons, titeg?

BLAIR. Sorry?

SEDDON. Transposing consonants — get it?

BLAIR (*faintly*). Ingenious.

SEDDON. The trick was that there were no rules as such. You had to do it like improvising music. It just needed a little tackpris but cos fork the cuffing ditios dookn't tag the feng tif of.

BLAIR. What?

SEDDON. Moo yee sot I wean: tackpris! Well too yot, Blair . . .

BLAIR. Yot?

SEDDON. You see — pick it up in no time! Come up to the belfry, I've got something up there which will interest you.

BLAIR. What?

SEDDON. Bats.

BLAIR. Bats in the belfry?

SEDDON. Had them for years without knowing it. I say, not that way . . .

BLAIR. Excuse me — I've got to find someone.

BLAIR *starts hurrying back down the stairs.*

SEDDON. Blair — ?

BLAIR. Terribly sorry — I really have to go.

He gallops down the stairs.

SEDDON (*distantly*). Blair . . . !

At the bottom of the stairs there is a collision.

BLAIR. I'm terribly sorry!

PURVIS. Blair!

BLAIR. Purvis! Thank goodness.

PURVIS. I'm very glad to see you.

BLAIR. I'm not sorry to see *you*. I'm damned if I can flush out anyone in authority. Where's the chap who's supposed to be running this show?

PURVIS. You mean Dr Seddon? I'll see if I can raise him for you.

BLAIR. Just as a courtesy . . . It was you I came to see, of course.

PURVIS. Really? That's awfully nice of you. I was about to have my constitutional. Care to accompany me?

BLAIR. Glad to give you a shove. Front door?

PURVIS. Can't do the steps. This way is better.

BLAIR. How do you feel?

PURVIS. Like a mermaid on wheels. Did I hurt your leg?

BLAIR. That wasn't you. Burnt my fingers pulling Pamela's forceps out of the fire, nearly knocked my Hilderson lantern clock off the mantle and got kicked by the donkey for my pains.

PURVIS. I'm awfully grateful to you for coming. It's impossible to have a sensible conversation with anyone in this place.

They move to the garden.

There's a path through the rhododendrons to a view of the sea.

BLAIR. Tip me off if we run into Seddon.

PURVIS. He's probably up in the bell tower collecting guano for the rose beds.

BLAIR. Quite a decent clock up there. Reminds me a little of St Giles's in Cambridge. If it's a turret movement I'd like to have a look at it. Did you say guano?

PURVIS. Yes. Seddon discovered a colony of bats up there the other day.

BLAIR. Bats in the belfry? Oh dear.

PURVIS. What's up?

BLAIR. Perhaps it would be better if I didn't see him. I'll drop him a note.

PURVIS. This is my favourite path. You can follow the top of the cliffs all the way round nearly to Cromer. At least you could if it wasn't for the wheelchair because of the boundary fence. Whoa!

BLAIR. Sorry.

PURVIS. Don't worry, this thing has got brakes. I don't come down this far if I'm on my own.

BLAIR. It *is* rather dangerous.

PURVIS. Not that. It's just a question of getting back up. You need strong wrists. There's a little flat bit to the side here, you could sit on that stump.

BLAIR. Fine. This is very pleasant. Do you mind if I pollute the atmosphere?

BLAIR *lights his pipe and sucks on it.*

Which way are we looking?

PURVIS. About north east. That's the Dogger Bank out there, over the horizon a bit . . . the scene of the last occasion on which Russian battle fleet engaged the British.

BLAIR. Really? When was that?

PURVIS. Ages ago. The Russian navy fired on some British trawlers.

BLAIR. Why?

PURVIS. It was a mistake. They thought the trawlers were Japanese torpedo boats.

BLAIR. In the North Sea?

PURVIS. As I said, it was a mistake. I think it was a bit foggy too.

BLAIR. It must have been.

PURVIS. It damned nearly led to war.

BLAIR. I should think it did.

PURVIS. The Tzar had to apologise to the King.

BLAIR. Oh . . .

PURVIS. Different Russia, of course.

BLAIR (*regretfully*). Yes, indeed.

PURVIS. They're getting there slowly.

BLAIR. Sorry?

PURVIS. Two steps forward, one and a half back. Narrowing the gap between rich and poor. That's what it's all about.

BLAIR. What?

PURVIS. Money, wealth.

BLAIR. I thought it was about freedom.

PURVIS. That's a luxury which has to be paid for. That's why the rich have always had it.

BLAIR. There's nothing in English law or the Constitution about what a man is worth.

PURVIS. There doesn't have to be. People only desire the freedom that is within their imagination. When you limit their horizon economically you limit their imagination. That's why the proletariat need the intellectuals — the failure of the masses to act is a failure of the mass imagination.

BLAIR. Purvis, what are you doing?

PURVIS. Just trying it out. How does it sound?

BLAIR. Like balderdash.

PURVIS. Really?

BLAIR. Doesn't it sound like balderdash to you?

PURVIS. Sometimes it does, sometimes it doesn't. That's my problem.

BLAIR. Well, we knew you had a problem, Purvis. What exactly is it?

PURVIS. Blair . . . you know how it is when you telephone someone and say, shall we meet at the Savoy Grill or Simpsons, and he says I don't mind, make it Simpsons if you like, or do you prefer the Savoy and you say no, that's fine, eight-thirty, and you hang up — and *suddenly* you think — did he say Simpsons or the Savoy? It's gone, you know. You've lost it. Well, that's what's happened to me.

BLAIR. The Savoy or Simpsons?

PURVIS. No, it isn't *really* like that, except that when you try to remember back, both ways sound equally right. I'm going back thirty-five years now, when I was still being run by Gell, or Rashnikov. Now Gell is dead and Rashnikov is probably dead too. They set me going between them like one of those pulley things one used to see in department stores, and they disappeared leaving me whizzing back and forth, back and forth, a canister between us and you, or us and them.

BLAIR. I didn't quite follow that last bit.

PURVIS. I remember some of it, no problem. I remember striking up a conversation with Rashnikov in one of the stacks in the Westminster library — political economy. Or perhaps he struck up a conversation with me. I remember having a few dinners with him, meeting some of his friends, arguing long into the night about politics, and I remember finally being asked to look something up for him in our back-numbers room in Whitehall . . . You remember that basement we used to have before we had microfilm? The thing he wanted was perfectly innocuous, but by that time, of course, I knew he was supposedly on the staff of the Soviet Commercial Attaché, so the next time he asked me to look something up, something which wasn't quite so innocuous, I of course reported the whole thing to Gell who was my superior.

BLAIR. Of course.

PURVIS. Sure enough, Gell told me to pretend to swallow the bait and to await instructions.

BLAIR. Straightforward enough.

PURVIS. It wasn't. Rashnikov was playing a subtle game. He had told me to tell Gell.

BLAIR. To tell him what?

PURVIS. To tell Gell that I was being recruited by Rashnikov. So that

Gell would be fooled into thinking that I was pretending to be
Rashnikov's man while I was really Gell's man.

BLAIR. Looking at it from Rashnikov's point of view.

PURVIS. Yes.

BLAIR. And did you tell Gell that this was going on, that Rashnikov
had told you to tell Gell?

PURVIS. Yes. I did. But . . .

BLAIR. But . . . ?

PURVIS. Well, I'm pretty sure that when I told Gell that all this was
going on, I was also acting on Rashnikov's instructions.

Pause.

BLAIR. But, if that were so, no doubt you told Gell that it *was* so.
No doubt you told Gell that Rashnikov had told you to tell Gell
that Rashnikov had told you to tell him that you were being
offered the bait.

PURVIS. That's what I can't remember. I've forgotten who is my
primary employer and who my secondary. For years I've
been feeding stuff in both directions, following my instructions
from either side, having been instructed to do so by the other, and
since each side wanted the other side to believe that I was working
for *it*, both sides were often giving me genuine stuff to pass on
to the other side . . . so the side I was actually working for became
. . . well, a matter of opinion really . . . it got lost.

Pause.

Blair?

BLAIR. I didn't speak.

PURVIS. Well, I just carried on doing what I was told . . . and one
day, not very long ago, I started thinking about my retirement.
The sherry party with the Chief. The presentation clock. The
London Transport senior citizens bus pass. The little dacha on the
Black Sea.

BLAIR. Purvis . . . ?

PURVIS. Exactly. Hang on a sec, I thought — hello! — which . . . ?
And blow me, I found I had forgotten.

BLAIR. But you worked for Gell. For *me*.

PURVIS. I worked for Rashnikov too.

BLAIR. Only because we asked you to play along.

PURVIS. *He* asked me to play along.

BLAIR. Let's not get into that again. You're one of us.

PURVIS. Well, I'd have to be, wouldn't I, to be of any use to him.

BLAIR. You're a churchwarden.

PURVIS. I thought about that but if one were covering up would one join a left-wing book club instead, for instance? Obviously not. Well, I suppose one might as a double bluff. Or, then again, one might not, as a triple bluff. I don't think I'm going to get to the bottom of this, to my infinite regress, I mean regret.

BLAIR. Oh —

PURVIS. Rashnikov said to me once, you've got to believe in the lie so strongly that even if you confessed they wouldn't believe you. Or was that Gell? One of the two.

BLAIR. All you've got to do is remember what you believed.

PURVIS. I remember I was very idealistic in those days, a real prig about Western decadence. On the other hand I was very patriotic and really didn't much care for foreigners. Obviously one scruple overcame the other, but as to whether it was the Savoy or Simpsons . . . At some point it must have ceased to matter to me. That's what I find so depressing. Did they tell you I was depressed? It's on my file here: Purvis is extremely depressed.

BLAIR. My dear chap . . .

PURVIS. Well, it *is* extremely depressing to find that one had turned into a canister. A hollow man. Like one of those Russian dolls — how appropriate! Yes, I'm like one of those sets of wooden dolls which fit into one another as they get smaller. Somewhere deep inside is the last doll, the only one which isn't hollow. At least, I suppose there is. There used to be. Perhaps I'm not even a set of dolls any more, perhaps I'm an onion. My idealism and my patriotism, folded on each other, having been peeled away leaving nothing in the middle except the lingering smell of onion.

BLAIR. Please don't cry.

PURVIS. I'm sorry. It's the onion. Oh stuff it, Blair!

BLAIR. That's the spirit. To the taxidermist with the lot of it.

   He sniffles. Pause.

PURVIS. Did you get the parrot by the way?

BLAIR. Oh yes. I'll let you have it back, of course.

PURVIS. I'd like you to keep it. Find a place for it in your folly.

BLAIR. Most kind of you. Well, I ought to be getting back.

PURVIS. Thank you for coming.

BLAIR. Let me give you a push up the hill.

PURVIS. No, I'll stay here for a while. I'll manage. I like looking at the sea.

BLAIR. As for that other matter . . . You never told Rashnikov anything which Gell hadn't told you to tell him, did you?

PURVIS. I never *knew* anything which Gell hadn't told me.

BLAIR. Well, there you are.

PURVIS. And I never knew anything to tell Gell which Rashnikov hadn't told me.

BLAIR. So the whole thing is rather academic, isn't it.

PURVIS. Thank you for understanding, Blair.

BLAIR. Cheerio, then.

PURVIS. Goodbye, Blair.

Scene Eight

A funeral service.

BLAIR. I thought I might find you here, Hogben. Still worrying?

HOGBEN. Yes, sir.

BLAIR. Too late to worry now.

HOGBEN. Too late for Purvis, you mean.

BLAIR. Alas, poor Purvis. We were all at fault, especially me.

HOGBEN. Why?

BLAIR. Well, one asks oneself . . . with the benefit of hindsight, was Clifftops the idea place to put a man who had a tendency to fling himself from a great height into a watery grave. Of course, one didn't realise it was a tendency, one thought it was a one-off, but even so . . . He certainly fooled me, the sly dog.

HOGBEN. You think he jumped?

BLAIR (*sighing*). What now?

HOGBEN. Just asking.

BLAIR. He wheeled. He rolled.

HOGBEN. Has anyone thought of checking the brakes on that wheelchair, sir?

BLAIR. The wheelchair has not surfaced, Hogben. Can you think of anyone who required Purvis's death, or even stood to gain by it?

HOGBEN. He had friends in High . . . (*The organ drowns him momentarily*.)

BLAIR. High places?

HOGBEN. Highgate. But then one would need to know more about that than I'm allowed to know. I don't know anything. I don't know what I'm doing here.

BLAIR. You're checking out the mourners. That's what you're doing here, Hogben. You smell a mystery. You're looking for a lead. And as is often the case after sudden death, a good place to start looking is the funeral. Any interesting mourners? Anybody unusual? Unexpected? Anybody who looks wrong? Too aloof? Too engaged? Too glamorous?

HOGBEN. I spotted her. Any idea who she is?

BLAIR. None. Have you spotted Hoskins?

HOGBEN. Hoskins?

BLAIR. Third from the end with the eyelashes.

Scene Nine

The churchyard. The VICAR *is saying goodbye to the mourners.*

VICAR. Goodbye . . . goodbye . . . sad occasion . . . would have been so pleased . . . goodbye . . . goodbye . . .

HOGBEN. Thank you, reverend. A beautiful service. The choristers in glorious voice . . .

VICAR. Thank you . . . Mr . . . ?

HOGBEN. Hogben.

VICAR. I noticed you at the back of the church, with the other gentleman. Were you colleagues of Mr Purvis's?

HOGBEN. Mr Blair is representing the firm. I was following in Purvis's footsteps. Perhaps I could walk along with you for a moment?

VICAR. I'm only going to the vicarage. We can take the side gate. We weren't quite sure what exactly Mr Purvis was doing.

HOGBEN. Quite. Incidentally, that lady in the dress with the fingernails . . .

VICAR. She lodged with Mr Purvis in Church Street. Quite innocently, of course. One has to make the point now-a-days, on the rare occasions when one is able to make it. I only met her once, a Turkish lady. She's a ballet dancer.

HOGBEN. Did you say ballet dancer or belly dancer?

VICAR. Ballet dancer. At least, I assumed she said ballet dancer. But now I come to think of it she does seem rather the wrong shape, and when I asked her where she danced she said Rotherhithe. Do you think she might possibly be a belly dancer?

HOGBEN. I'd put money on it. Let me hold the gate for you.

VICAR. Would you care for a spot of cheese?

HOGBEN. Thank you very much.

Scene Ten

In the VICAR's *house.*

VICAR. Try this one, Mr Hogben. This is a Caerphilly.

HOGBEN (*with his mouth full*). Welsh? I was going to ask you —

VICAR. Hardly any Caerphilly made in Wales any more — mostly in Somerset. A hundred years ago every farm house in that part of South Wales made its own cheese. A hundred and fifty years ago — what do you think?

HOGBEN. I don't know.

VICAR. It wasn't made at all! It's a newcomer, invented for the miners, makes an ideal meal underground, doesn't dry up, very digestible, and you can make it in two or three hours using hardly more than its own weight in milk. A cheddar needs ten times its own weight in milk.

HOGBEN. I like toasted cheese. Welse Rarebit. Incidentally, Purvis mentioned —

VICAR. Now your cheese for Welsh rarebit is Red Leicester. It'll never be so fine as a Cheshire because it doesn't go on maturing the same way, it's ready at three months, good for nine, finished at a year. But it's the best English cheese for melting. The orange colour is a tint, of course — carrot juice originally, but since the eighteenth century tinted with *annatto,* an extract from the *Bixa Orellana* tree from the West Indies. You need one dram to every two and a half gallons of milk.

HOGBEN. Amazing.

VICAR. I'm always glad to meet a man who appreciates cheese.

HOGBEN. Did Purvis appreciate cheese . . . on toast perhaps?

VICAR. One doesn't like to speak ill of the dead, but I tell you now that Purvis may have liked the odd piece of cheese but he knew nothing about it, nothing at all. Purvis was a man who would melt an *epoisses* on a slice of Mother's Pride as soon as look at you.

HOGBEN. An *epoisses*?

VICAR. Purvis blamed the choir, but I'm not convinced. You would have really liked my *epoisses*. I brought it back from Dijon. I chose one which had been renneted with fennel. The curd is milled, salted and then refined on rye straw. As soon as the mould starts forming the cheese is soaked in *Marc de Bourgogne*, an eau de vie distilled from local grape pulp. A beautiful thing, brick red on the outside, of course.

HOGBEN. Of course.

VICAR. I put it in the vestry because it can't abide central heating. That was a Friday.

HOGBEN. Don't tell me Purvis . . . ?

VICAR. Cut a great wedge out of it. The electric grill was still warm. I held up Matins for ten minutes while I searched the vestry for evidence.

HOGBEN. Did you find any?

VICAR. A half eaten rarebit in Purvis's hymn book.

HOGBEN. An unsavoury business.

Scene Eleven

BLAIR's *house. Clocks chiming and striking. They signal one o'clock. There is a spread of several seconds between them.*

PAMELA. Come and sit down, Giles. Soup's getting cold.

BLAIR *grunts.*

Are you going back to the office after lunch?

BLAIR. I suppose so.

PAMELA. Your funeral seems to have got you down.

BLAIR. It wasn't exactly *my* funeral.

PAMELA. Well, don't stand there brooding and looking out at the rain. What's worrying you?

BLAIR. Just thinking . . . I could have had a rustic pagoda.

A late clock strikes the hour.

The Graham bracket isn't itself, it's sickening for something. I'm pretty sure I know what it is. I'll have a look at it at the weekend. I think I've run out of copper sheeting . . . if I write down what I need could you pick some up for me from that place in Pimlico?

PAMELA. Must I?

BLAIR. It would be quite convenient for you, if you are in the vicinity, it's practically next door to Eaton Square.

PAMELA. Proximity and convenience aren't necessarily the same thing. Well, I'll try to fit it in.

The doorbell.

Are you expecting someone?

BLAIR. Half expecting. I'll go and see.

He goes through a door.

Don't worry Mrs Ryan, I'll get it!

He opens the front door.

Come in, Hogben.

HOGBEN. I'm sorry to . . .

BLAIR. It's all right, I was half expecting you.

HOGBEN. Only half?

BLAIR. I was half expecting you to come here and half expecting you to telephone me to meet you in the park.

He closes the door.

Come in.

HOGBEN. Thank you, sir.

BLAIR *closes a second door.*

BLAIR. An interesting little funeral.

HOGBEN. Yes. I hardly know where to begin.

BLAIR. You talked to the vicar, of course.

HOGBEN. Yes.

BLAIR. A parochial scandal, as scandals go. I don't think for a moment that Purvis was guilty.

HOGBEN. Of what, exactly, Mr Blair?

BLAIR. Purvis wasn't your left wing book club type who would do down his vicar.

HOGBEN. What type was Purvis?

BLAIR. I would say he was loyal.

HOGBEN. Did you know he had an invitation to Buckingham Palace? To a garden party?

BLAIR. Yes. As a matter of fact I rather put it his way. The department was due for one and, speaking for myself, I don't get much of a thrill anymore from queuing up for a cup of tea and a fancy cake.

HOGBEN. He was going to take his lodger. She was most disappointed that the invitation was not transferable.

BLAIR. The belly dancer?

HOGBEN. Exactly. I said there was something funny about Purvis's letter. And that's what it was — it's all true.

BLAIR. Well, of course.

PAMELA. Giles —

BLAIR. Darling, this is Mr Hogben, a policeman. My wife, Pamela . . .

HOGBEN (*overcome with embarrassment*). Oh . . . how do you do . . . Mrs Blair . . .

PAMELA. How do you do, Mr Hogben — please sit down.

HOGBEN. Thank you — oh! Sorry! I'm *terribly* sorry! I sat on your parrot.

PAMELA. It's not as bad as it looks, he was already dead. Giles, do remove him. I've given up on lunch. I'm off to see Don Juan — he hasn't been getting his oats. See you later perhaps, Mr Hogben.

She leaves, closing the door.

BLAIR. You were saying.

HOGBEN. Yes. I'm awfully sorry.

BLAIR. What about?

HOGBEN. Your wife and Don Juan.

BLAIR (*perplexed*). What?

HOGBEN. Look, sir, if everything in Purvis's letter is true . . .

BLAIR. Oh, it's true all right.

HOGBEN. It's a situation. A bit of a bombshell.

BLAIR. Oh, come now. What sort of fool do you take me for?

HOGBEN. You mean you knew it was true?

BLAIR. Of course. One mustn't get over dramatic about these things. One must try to be civilised about them. Keep them in the family.

HOGBEN. But surely, sir . . . the head of Q6 . . . an opium den in his own house. . .

BLAIR. Oh, *that*. That's a different matter. On that subject I would be inclined to say . . . that one mustn't get over dramatic about these things.

HOGBEN. Over dramatic? I don't see how one can be over dramatic. You asked me a few days ago who might want Purvis out of the way. It looks as if the answer is your Chief.

BLAIR. Why? I don't follow.

HOGBEN. An opium den in Eaton Square?

BLAIR. Hogben, you're in danger of making yourself look foolish. Too many tuppenny dreadfulls in your childhood reading. You and Purvis. A shiver of delicious horror runs right through your Farnham Royal morality. Opium den! The quintessence of moral depravity combined with dubious foreign habits. The Chief stoned to the eyeballs in a brocade dressing gown, beating a gong when he is ready for the other half. Look, I've been in his den. T.V., hi-fi, books, writing desk, dead animals poking their heads out of the walls, Axminster on the floor. It's not an opium den, it's a *den*. And to him, enjoying an occasional pipe would be simply a souvenir of a Far Eastern posting. Something brought home in the baggage like a carved ivory elephant. It isn't some ghastly secret for which you drive all the way to Cromer in order to tamper with the brakes of a wheelchair. You really are absurd, Hogben.

HOGBEN. Are you trying to tell me to forget all about it?

BLAIR. Certainly not. You must make your report and give it to your Chief.

HOGBEN. That's what I intend to do. Mr Wren may have a different attitude.

BLAIR. I doubt it. In any case, if I were you I wouldn't bother Mr Wren with your murder story.

HOGBEN. Why?

BLAIR. Because I had another farewell letter from Purvis.

Scene Twelve

PURVIS (*reads*). Dear Blair. Well, goodbye again, assuming that I don't fall into a fishing boat. Please don't feel badly. Suicide is no more than a trick played on the calendar. You may like to know that whether or not I left the fold all those years ago when my intellect aspired to rule my actions, I found at the end that my remaining affinity was with the English character, a curious bloom which at Clifftops merely appears in its overblown form. Looking around at the people I've rubbed up against, I see that with the significant exception of my friend in Highgate they all inhabit a sort of Clifftops catchment area: if we lowered our entry qualifications we would be inundated. I find this reassuring. I realise I am where I belong, at last, even though, in common with

all the other inmates, I have the impression that I am here by mistake while understanding perfectly why everybody else should be here. In this respect Clifftops has an effect precisely opposite to being in a Marxist discussion group. I'm grateful to you for our chat. It led me to think about Gell and the way he used to wear hunting pink to the office in the season, and the way he used to complain about not being able to eat asparagus without dripping the butter after the first time he broke his neck, and I thought I *couldn't* have lied to Gell, not to Gell, not for a mere conviction. The man was so much himself that one would have been betraying him instead of the system. I hope I'm right, though I would settle for *knowing* that I'm wrong. Oddly enough, my friend from Highgate came to visit me, or rather to meet me at the boundary fence, and he tells me that the reason Rashnikov disappeared was that he had been recalled under suspicion of having been duped by Gell and me. Rashnikov said there was a logical reason why this should have been the impression given, but unfortunately he died of a brainstorm while trying to work it out. You might say that the same happened to me. My regards to your good lady.
Yours sincerely, Rupert Purvis.

Scene Thirteen

The CHIEF's *den. A cosy atmosphere. All three men are smoking pipes.*

BLAIR. There is something else, sir.

CHIEF. Yes. This dog. Now let's be reasonable about this, Wren. Quite unexpectedly the bargee has sent in a bill for three hundred pounds, claiming that his wretched dog was a member of the Kennel Club and runner up in his class in the South of England Show. Is that correct, Blair?

BLAIR. Quite correct, sir, but . . .

WREN. I don't dispute any of that. I'm only saying that the dog was killed, in effect, by Q6, not by Q9.

CHIEF. We killed him but your man Hogben filed the report confirming the dog's death as an incident during *his own case.* All the paper work is Q9, and, crucially, the bill for the dog was sent to Q9.

WREN. Look, I'm good for fifty if it helps. I'll put it in under dog handling. I suppose Hogben must have handled the dog.

CHIEF. Let's go halves. One-fifty each.

BLAIR. Excuse me, sir. Why can't we use Purvis's money? After all, he killed the dog.

CHIEF. Purvis's money?

BLAIR. Highgate kept giving him odd sums for film and bus fares, which we made him accept to preserve his credibility, and which Highgate made him declare for the same reason. There must be several hundred pounds by now, lying in some account somewhere.

CHIEF. Excellent. Well thought, Blair. Would you care for a pipe?

BLAIR. No thank you, sir. I'll stick to the old briar.

CHIEF. How is your pipe, Wren. Ready for another?

WREN. No thanks, it's bubbling along very nicely.

CHIEF. Jolly good. Well, that's that.

BLAIR. Actually it wasn't about the dog. It was about the opium. And your . . . your private life generally. Purvis said it was all over Highgate. I'd like to know how it got there.

CHIEF. Purvis took it up there. I put it into his Highgate package a couple of months ago. He was coming up for retirement and I thought if they thought they had something on *me* I might get a tickle as his replacement . . . Nothing doing so far. Perhaps it's just as well. These double and triple bluffs can get to be a bit of a headache. It got to be a bit of a headache for Purvis.

WREN. How did it work?

The CHIEF *speaks, slowly, deliberately, reflectively; the pauses filled with the gentle bubbling of his pipe.*

CHIEF. Well, in the beginning the idea was that if they thought that we knew that they thought Purvis was their man . . . they would assume that the information we gave Purvis to give to them . . . would be information designed to *mislead* . . . so they would take that into account . . . and, thus, if we told Purvis to tell them that we were going to do something . . . they would draw the conclusion that we were *not* going to do it . . . but as we were on to that, we naturally were giving Purvis genuine information to give to them, knowing that they would be drawing the wrong conclusions from it . . . This is where it gets tricky . . . because if they kept drawing these wrong conclusions while the other thing kept happening . . . they would realise that we had got to Purvis first after all . . . So to keep Purvis in the game we would have to *not* do some of the things which Purvis told them we *would* be doing, even though our first reason for telling Purvis was that we did intend to do them . . . In other words . . . in order to keep fooling the Russians, we had to keep doing the opposite of what we really wanted to do . . . Now this is where it gets *extremely* tricky . . . Obviously we couldn't keep doing the opposite of what we wished to do simply to keep Purvis in the game . . . so we frequently had to give Purvis the wrong information from which the Russians would draw the right conclusion, which enabled us to do what we wished to do, although the Russians, thanks to Purvis, knew we were going to do it . . .

In other words, Purvis was acting, in effect, as a genuine Russian spy in order to maintain his usefulness as a bogus Russian spy . . . The only reason why this wasn't entirely disastrous for us was that, of course, during the whole of this time, the Russians, believing us to believe that Purvis was in their confidence, had been giving Purvis information designed to mislead *us* . . . and in order to maintain Purvis's credibility they have been forced to do some of the things which they told Purvis they *would* do, although their first reason for telling him was they didn't wish to do them. (*Pause*.) In other words, if Purvis's mother had got kicked by a horse things would be more or less exactly as they are now.

Pause.

If I were Purvis I'd drown myself.

Sea sounds.

PURVIS. P.S. Incidentally, Blair, Dr Seddon thinks that you ought to be in Clifftops yourself, but I'll leave you to field that one.

Slowly fade out sea.

AUTUMN SUNSHINE

by William Trevor

William Trevor was born in Mitchelstown, County Cork, in 1928 and spent his childhood in provincial Ireland. He attended a number of Irish schools and later Trinity College, Dublin. He is a member of the Irish Academy of Letters. His many books include *The Old Boys* (Hawthornden Prize), *The Boarding-House, The Love Department, The Day We Got Drunk on Cake, Mrs Eckdorf in O'Neill's Hotel, Miss Gomez and the Brethren, The Ballroom of Romance and Other Stories, Elizabeth Alone, Angels at the Ritz* (winner of the Royal Society of Literature Award in 1975), *The Children of Dynmouth* (Whitbread Award), *Lovers of Their Time, Other People's Worlds, Beyond the Pale* and *Fools of Fortune*. In 1976 he received the Allied Irish Banks' prize and in 1977 was awarded the CBE in recognition of his valuable services to Literature. His work for radio includes *Beyond the Pale*, which was a Giles Cooper Award winner in 1980. William Trevor is married and has two sons.

Autumn Sunshine was first broadcast on BBC Radio 3 on 2nd November 1982. The cast was as follows:

CANON MORAN	John Welsh
UNA	Susie Kelly
CARLEY, *her husband*	Kevin Flood
EMMA	Roisin Donaghy
THOMAS, *her husband* } WILLOUGHBY	Mark Mulholland
LINDA	Stella McCusker
JOHN, *her husband*	John Hewitt
SLATTERY	Ian McElhinney
OWNER OF PUBLIC HOUSE } MRS DAVIS	Catherine Gibson
DEIRDRE	Deirdre Donnelly
MRS ROCHE } MRS O'NEILL	Margaret D'Arcy
HAROLD	Tony McEwan
NEWSCASTER	Paddy Scully
PARISHIONERS	Roisin Donaghy, Stella McCusker John Hewitt, Ian McElhinney
PIANIST	Philip Hammond

Director Robert Cooper

The 'Schubert' referred to in the text is a piece of piano music which Frances Moran played in her lifetime.

A rural graveyard in Co. Wexford. It is morning, eleven-thirty on an autumn day. The coffin of Frances Moran has been lowered into an open grave. CANON MORAN *conducts the service. The mourners consist of three of* CANON MORAN's *daughters, their husbands and children, as well as all his parishioners.*

CANON MORAN. . . . O holy and merciful Saviour, thou most worthy judge eternal, suffer us not, at our last hour, for any pains of death, to fall from thee.

A handful of clay rattles on the surface of the coffin. UNA *and* EMMA *weep a little.*

CANON MORAN. For as much as it has pleased Almighty God of his great mercy to take unto himself the soul of our dear sister here departed, we therefore commit her body to the ground; earth to earth, ashes to ashes, dust to dust . . .

The beginning of Schubert's 'Impromptu in B flat', very lightly. Fade.

CANON MORAN. . . . The grace of our Lord Jesus Christ, and the love of God, and the fellowship of the Holy Ghost, be with us all evermore.

MOURNERS. Amen.

Silence.

Fade up lunchtime sounds in the rectory.

JOHN. Old Willoughby was looking well.

CANON MORAN. He's better than he was. (*Pause.*) D'you remember, Una — it must be twenty years ago — that argument he had with Eugene Ryan. Grazing rights? D'you remember that?

UNA. Grazing? Now, wasn't that — ?

CANON MORAN. Your mother sorted it out. I was never much good at that kind of thing.

EMMA. There was Mrs Tobin's skirt: I remember that.

CANON MORAN. Yes.

EMMA. Mrs Tobin was seen with a skirt on her, John, that appeared to be an altar cloth from St Michael's.

LINDA. Oh, it *was* an altar cloth. I mean, the altar cloth was gone and there was Mrs Tobin with all this lovely embroidery around her.

JOHN *and* THOMAS *politely laugh.*

JOHN. I heard that one before.

THOMAS. So did I.

CANON MORAN. Frances was marvellous at things like that. Mrs Tobin was one of Father Hayes's, you understand — well, so was Eugene Ryan. It might have been tricky, but it never was. Father Hayes adored her.

A melancholy note has been struck, the old man is about to drift into a reverie. UNA *and* EMMA *distribute cheerfulness.*

UNA. Tobin Below, Mrs Tobin's husband was always known as.

EMMA. Because he —

UNA. Why was that, Father? Why was Mr Tobin known as Tobin Below?

CANON MORAN. Oh. Because his cottage was the other side of the Boharbawn crossroads. There used to be another Tobin at the top of the hill. (*He drifts back into his reverie again, and out of it.*) And then of course there was Alice Pratt. Heaven knows what would have become of Alice Pratt if it hadn't been for Frances.

CARLEY. What did become of her, Canon?

CANON MORAN. Frances and Father Hayes persuaded the man to marry her. They've got eleven now. They all go to Father Hayes, but Alice still comes to me. Was she there this morning?

LINDA. Yes, she was there.

CANON MORAN. She thought the world of Frances.

UNA. More ham, Father?

CANON MORAN. No, no. Thank you, Una.

LINDA. I'll make some tea.

CANON MORAN. I'd love a cup of tea.

*A thought suddenly occurs to him, a thought which always
occurred to his wife when one of their daughters came to the
rectory. It pleases him to remember to offer what she would have
offered.*

CANON MORAN. What would you like from the garden? To take
back to Dublin?

LINDA. Oh no, Father, not at all.

CANON MORAN. You must have something.

Rectory sounds fade.

Fade up garden sounds.

UNA. You'll be all right?

CANON MORAN. I have my daughters.

UNA. We're a long way away. I wish you'd think —

CANON MORAN. I belong here. I couldn't not go on. (*Pause.*) You'll
come quite often? All of you?

UNA. Of course we will.

CANON MORAN. Don't say I need a housekeeper because I'm not
going to have one. (*Pause.*) She's still here, you know.

UNA. Yes.

CANON MORAN. Autumn was her favourite time. Look, those
lettuces there aren't bad.

He moves away from UNA, *to cut a few heads of lettuce.* UNA
calls after him.

UNA. Not too many now. Leave some for yourself.

*Fade up very faintly — as if coming over a great distance — the
echo of the Schubert in* CANON MORAN's *imagination.*
CANON MORAN *breathes heavily as he bends down to cut the
lettuces.* UNA *calls out.*

UNA. Deirdre doesn't know?

CANON MORAN. I wrote to her.

UNA (*surprised*). But there's no address. We'd have written ourselves
if we'd had an address.

CANON MORAN. There was an old one. Years ago. A letter might
be forwarded. Now!

He gives her the lettuces.

UNA. Oh, they're lovely. Lovely and fresh. But you've given us far too
many.

CANON MORAN. Share them up among you.

They begin their walk back from the vegetable garden to the front of the house, where the others are sitting in the sun.

CANON MORAN. In a way I wish Deidre had married. At least you know where you are when your daughters have married. (*Pause.*) Your mother used to say that.

UNA (*laughing slightly*). While you said that no one was good enough for any of us.

CANON MORAN. Your mother was wiser about such things. (*Laughing also.*) Yet I was meant to be the brainy one.

UNA. I suppose Deidre *may* have married, you know.

CANON MORAN. No. No, I think she would have told us that.

They walk on. There's a pause in their conversation. The sound of the others' conversation at the front of the house can now be heard.

UNA. Father, there's Mother's music, it's still open on the piano and there's her clothes: before we go we could —

CANON MORAN. No. No, I must do that myself.

The conversation sound becomes louder as they approach. It ceases abruptly, as if interrupted by the sound of CANON MORAN *opening Frances's wardrobe. The door creaks.*

Silence. Only the CANON's *breathing.*

The dresses in the wardrobe rustle, coat-hangers jangling. Very faintly again, the Schubert.

CANON MORAN. O Lord, give me strength . . .

Slowly he closes the creaking wardrobe door, unable to sort Frances's clothes out just now.

CANON MORAN. Your fingerprints are still here. All over the rectory, oh my darling. There's nothing I'll ever do again without remembering being with you. And most of all in autumn. I should have known that you would die in autumn . . .

It is the next morning.

The postman's car crunches over the gravel, halts. CANON MORAN *is cutting the front lawn with a push-mower.* SLATTERY, *the postman, gets out of the car. He whistles as he approaches* CANON MORAN — *'Phil the fluter's ball'.*

  CANON MORAN *takes the letters and the 'Irish Times'.*

CANON MORAN. There you are, Slattery.

SLATTERY. Isn't that a great bit of weather, Canon? We're set for a while, would you say?

CANON MORAN. I hope so certainly.

SLATTERY. Ah, we surely are, sir.

CANON MORAN. How's the fishing, Slattery?

SLATTERY. I'd have brought you a few if I'd caught any, Canon.

CANON MORAN. No, no, I didn't mean —

SLATTERY. Ah, I know you didn't of course, sir. I'll maybe go out again tonight. If it wasn't for the darkness coming in it's a great time of year for it.

CANON MORAN. And Mrs Slattery's leg? Is she a bit more comfortable?

SLATTERY. She's coming out of the plaster today, Canon.

CANON MORAN. Ah, well, that's great.

SLATTERY. There's a bit more trouble I see there on your paper. Poor devil in Armagh, got into his car . . .

CANON MORAN. Oh dear, dear . . .

SLATTERY. Blown to smithereens.

CANON MORAN. Oh, my goodness . . .

SLATTERY. Ah, 'twould depress you. Then again you have your man leading out another march, provoking more trouble with it. (*He sighs heavily.*) Well, I'd best be on the road. Cheerio so, sir.

CANON MORAN. Good-bye, Slattery.

  The van drives off.

  CANON MORAN'S *'Irish Times' rattles as he pauses where* SLATTERY *has left him, reading about the tragedy. He sighs himself.*

CANON MORAN. At least you're spared all that.

He crosses the gravel, back to his lawn-mower, opening his letters on the way. He stops suddenly, excitedly addresses his dead wife.

CANON MORAN. Deirdre! My dear, it's from Deirdre! Deirdre's written.

DEIRDRE'S VOICE. I'm sorry. I couldn't stop crying actually. I've never known anyone as nice or as generous as she was. For ages I didn't even want to believe she was dead. I went on imagining her in the rectory, and doing the flowers in church and shopping in Enniscorthy.

CANON MORAN. Oh, Deirdre . . .

DEIRDRE'S VOICE. Well, I'm coming back for a little while now. if you could put up with me and wouldn't find it too much. I'll cross over to Rosslare on the 29th, the morning crossing, and then I'll come on to Enniscorthy on the bus. I don't know what time it will be but there's a pub just by where the bus drops you so could we meet in the small bar there at six o'clock and then I won't have to lug my cases too far? I hope you won't mind going into such a place. If you can't make it or don't want to see me it's understandable, so if you don't turn up by half six I'll see if I can get a bus on up to Dublin. Only I need to get back to Ireland for a while. Love, Deirdre.

CANON MORAN (*whispering*). Love, Deirdre. (*Pause.*) Love, Deirdre.

Elated, delighted, he again addresses Frances.

CANON MORAN. Oh, Frances. Please God you know this.

Radio Eireann on the wireless of the lounge-bar where CANON MORAN *is to await the arrival of his daughter: popular music, advertisements, popular music again. Fade to background as* CANON MORAN *enters and some traffic noise is heard from the street outside. The door closes, the traffic is no longer heard. The landlady of the pub is surprised to find a clergyman on her premises. She knows* CANON MORAN *by sight but cannot quite place him. Her voice reflects her surprise, though she tries to keep it friendly.*

WOMAN. Good evening to you, sir. And a lovely one outside, isn't it?

CANON MORAN. It is. It is.

He feels a little awkward and out of place. There is no one else in the lounge-bar.

WOMAN. It does your heart good, a sunny autumn. I was saying that to himself at dinnertime.

CANON MORAN. Ah yes, yes.

WOMAN. Sir down, sir. Come in for a rest, have you? Is there a drink at all I can get you? (*Hastily*.) No need for anything, sir, just take your ease if it's how you'd prefer it.

CANON MORAN. I'm meeting my daughter off the Wexford 'bus.

WOMAN. You're as welcome as the day is long, sir. I'll leave you a minute now, only I have himself in the kitchen shouting his head off for his tea.

CANON MORAN. It's very kind of you.

WOMAN. The old wireless'll be company for you.

She goes, turning up the radio volume. The news has just begun.

NEWSCASTER. . . . found to be dead on arrival at the hospital. The carrier-bag was left in a corner of the public house, hidden by a piano. (*Pause.*) Israeli fighter-jets have again —

DEIRDRE. Father!

CANON MORAN. Deirdre! Deirdre!

DEIRDRE (*in an excited rush*). Oh, I'm sorry to be late like this. I didn't know that you'd be here. I didn't know what to expect.

NEWSCASTER. . . . In a conflicting report the Syrians claim to have lost only a single plane, while inflicting heavy damages on Israeli targets.

The wireless is abruptly turned off as the WOMAN *enters the bar again.*

WOMAN. Good evening, miss. You got here safely then.

DEIRDRE. Yes, thank you. Yes. Father, will we have a drink, now that we're here? Would you mind? I'm exhausted after all that train and boat and bus and —

CANON MORAN. Of course. Of course.

WOMAN. What'll I get you then? Sure, you'd be dropping dead with travel the way it is these days. Did you come far, miss? England, is it?

DEIRDRE. London. I'd like a whiskey. A John Jameson, please. Father . . . ?

CANON MORAN. Well, I don't think I'll have —

DEIRDRE *speaks in a low, almost conspiritorial, voice to the* WOMAN.

DEIRDRE. Bring my father a mineral, will you?

WOMAN. I surely will, miss. Sit yourself down now and I'll carry them over to you. Ah no, leave those cases where they are — there won't be anyone in here for an hour.

DEIRDRE *sits down at the table beside her father.*

DEIRDRE (*quietly*). I didn't know if you'd turn up. I thought afterwards a public house in Enniscorthy wasn't quite the place to meet you.

CANON MORAN. Of course I'd come. Of course, dear. Of course.

DEIRDRE. I haven't treated you very well.

CANON MORAN. The past's past, Deirdre.

The WOMAN *places their two glasses on the table.*

WOMAN. Now.

The rattle of money as CANON MORAN *pays.*

WOMAN. Another ten, sir. Lovely, that's lovely.

DEIRDRE. I'm sorry I didn't write immediately.

CANON MORAN. You explained in your letter, Deirdre.

DEIRDRE. It was ages before I knew. It was an old address you sent your letter to.

CANON MORAN. I guessed. (*Pause.*) I'd have met you off the boat, you know. There was no need for you to go taking the bus.

DEIRDRE. I didn't want to bother you with that.

CANON MORAN. Oh now, it isn't far, Deirdre.

There is an awkward silence. DEIRDRE *drinks.*

DEIRDRE. Is it all right — d'you mind if I smoke?

CANON MORAN. Oh, no, no. No, it's quite all right.

DEIRDRE *lights a cigarette.*

CANON MORAN. I have grapes for Mrs Roche.

DEIRDRE. Grapes?

CANON MORAN. We've always sold the grapes, this time of year: don't you remember?

DEIRDRE (*softly*). No. No, I don't actually.

CANON MORAN. Mrs Roche. In Slaney Street.

DEIRDRE. Is the old picture-house still there? Halfway up that hill. Grey cement.

CANON MORAN. No. That's all changed.

DEIRDRE. I remember cycling home from it. Not able to keep up with Una and Linda and Emma.

CANON MORAN. You know you have nieces and nephews now? And brothers-in-law you've never met?

DEIRDRE (*vaguely; uninterested*). Oh yes. (*Pause*). I wish I'd seen her just once again.

CANON MORAN. She'd like to have seen you too.

DEIRDRE. You miss her dreadfully, of course.

CANON MORAN. I miss her. As if the greater part of myself has gone. She wasn't only a person I loved, nor just a helpmeet to me. She knew about the world the way I never could: I was always at a loss when something went wrong and, you know, she never was. She knew so much; she had a kind of *faith* in human frailty. She saw it everywhere: it was the weakness in people, she used to say, that made them what they were, as much as strength did.

Silence.

DEIRDRE *does not attempt to comment on these observations. She drinks, replaces her glass on the table.*

CANON MORAN (*gently laughing*). She used to say her own weakness was for clothes. She overreached herself whenever she went to Dublin, coming back penniless. (*Pause.*) I can still hear her playing, you know. It echoes all over the rectory, as if she wants to be a ghost for me but it's all too soon.

DEIRDRE. Now, now, you mustn't think about . . .

CANON MORAN. Oh, I'm not melancholy. I only hope she knows you've come back for a while. Will we take the grapes over now?

Bring up traffic noise, the CANON'*s car drawing up outside* MRS ROCHE'*s shop. During the conversation which follows — on the street outside* MRS ROCHE'*s shop — the car engine runs.*

MRS ROCHE. Well, I'd never have guessed. I'd never know you, Deirdre.

CANON MORAN. She's returned for a little while, Mrs Roche. There you are then. Five chips full.

MRS ROCHE. Oh, they're lovely. Lovely. Come in now and we'll fix up what I owe you, Canon.

CANON MORAN. No, no we'll leave it till next time if you don't mind, Mrs Roche. Deirdre's very tired after her journey. We'll get back to the rectory, I think.

DEIRDRE. Nice to see you, Mrs Roche. Nice to be in Enniscorthy again.

MRS ROCHE. Ah, the dear bless you. (*Lowering her voice*.) Look after him now. It's a lonely life he's left with.

The car door bangs as the CANON *gets in. He puts the car into gear.* MRS ROCHE *calls out above the noise of the engine.*

MRS ROCHE. Goodbye now, Canon. Goodbye, Deirdre.

DEIRDRE. Goodbye, Mrs Roche.

The car draws away.

The clatter of china and cutlery as DEIRDRE *and her father have supper in the rectory.*

DEIRDRE. Did you worry?

CANON MORAN. Well . . . I suppose we did. A bit. (*Pause.*) We got your picture postcard from Fishguard.

DEIRDRE. But what on earth can you have thought? I said I'd gone to stay with Maeve Coles in Cork.

CANON MORAN. I know. It was a shock.

DEIRDRE. I didn't know whether to send you another card or not, saying I'd found work so's you wouldn't worry. Would it be worse to hear I was working in an egg-packing station? Would it be a horrible disappointment? I wondered.

CANON MORAN. No, we were glad to get that card too. (*Pause.*) What have you done since, Deirdre?

DEIRDRE. Well, there was a while in a place that made plastic ear-phones. And then a cleaning job near Euston, a hotel that was. And then a year with Use-Us Office Cleansing Services.

CANON MORAN. Use-Us — But you can't have liked any of that work, Deirdre?

DEIRDRE *lights a cigarette.*

DEIRDRE. No. None of it. (*Suddenly becoming rather intense.*) I'm sorry. I'm sorry I spoilt everything at the rectory, the happy family we were: I had no right to do that.

CANON MORAN. Oh, but you didn't, my dear. Of course you didn't.

DEIRDRE. What did you think? Both of you? What did you say to one another about the daughter who didn't fit in?

CANON MORAN. We didn't . . .

DEIRDRE. Tell me.

CANON MORAN. You were always special because you were the youngest, Deirdre. We thought we'd finished with having children. We thought maybe — maybe we'd somehow or other given you too much love. In gratitude because you had been born.

DEIRDRE. Yes, I always felt I was the favourite. Yours in particular.

CANON MORAN. I'm afraid you were.

DEIRDRE. I'll never forget your reading to me, how I would bother you, bearing down on you with a book. And you were never cross.

CANON MORAN. It's nice you're back, Deirdre.

DEIRDRE *hesitates before she speaks again.*

DEIRDRE. Her clothes —

CANON MORAN. I told Una I'd see to them myself.

DEIRDRE. And have you?

CANON MORAN. No. (*Pause.*) They should be given away. Mrs O'Neill, I suppose: she has various charities.

DEIRDRE. Let me see to it for you.

CANON MORAN. Una wanted to, but — Yes, all right.

DEIRDRE. And your washing? Your laundry? Who does that for you?

CANON MORAN (*very surprised*). Mrs Dwyer. In Boharbawn. You probably don't —

DEIRDRE. You have to bring it to her? No one comes here? To clean or anything like that?

CANON MORAN. I drop it in to her. Slattery sometimes takes it.

DEIRDRE. Slattery?

CANON MORAN. The postman. (*Pause.*) It works perfectly well.

DEIRDRE. I see.

CANON MORAN *rises, his chair rasping on the linoleum of the floor.*

CANON MORAN. Will we take a walk about the garden? Go down to the river maybe?

Country sounds, river, etc.

DEIRDRE. What are they like, the husbands?

CANON MORAN. The . . . ?

DEIRDRE. Una's, Emma's, Linda's.

CANON MORAN. Well . . .

DEIRDRE. Please tell me.

CANON MORAN. Emma's Thomas is a farmer. Sizeable acreage in Co Meath, he doesn't say an awful lot. A dependable smile, your mother used to say.

DEIRDRE. But not the kind to end up with after years of being choosey? Which Emma always was.

CANON MORAN. Oh, no, I don't mean that at all. Thomas is kindness itself. And Emma loves him, which is all that matters.

DEIRDRE. And Linda's John?

CANON MORAN. Wiry and suave, making his way in the Bank of Ireland. He has a little orange-coloured moustache; he's good at golf. Linda's ambitious for him: she'd like to see him manager in Limerick or Galway.

DEIRDRE. Yes, Linda did have an ambitious streak. And Una's Carley?

CANON MORAN. Well, older of course. He's an importer of tea and wine, and I dare say he looks it. Flushed and stout and well-to-do.

DEIRDRE. You give your daughters up reluctantly, don't you?

CANON MORAN (*laughing*). My particular frailty, your mother used to say. To set against her extravagance. (*Pause. More seriously.*) Yes, I do give them up reluctantly. It isn't generous of me. Thomas is good-natured, she used to reassure me. But Thomas seemed to me to be the boy at the back of the class, the farmer's son who became a good judge of beef cattle. John's fun, she said, he always has a joke to tell, but I could never help feeling that John was a bit of a whippersnapper. Carley laid his success at Una's feet, but Carley could almost be her father.

DEIRDRE. But surely, now —

CANON MORAN. Oh, it's all right now. I quite accept them now.

They continue their walk, not speaking for a while.

DEIRDRE. I have a friend. Someone who's been good to me.

CANON MORAN. Who's that?

DEIRDRE. Someone called Harold.

Again they walk without conversing.

DEIRDRE. I want to tell you about Harold, Father. I want you to meet him.

CANON MORAN. Yes, of course.

DEIRDRE. We have a lot in common, I mean, he's the only person . . .

She hesitates, falters.

CANON MORAN. Are you fond of him, Deirdre?

DEIRDRE. Yes, I am.

Another silence gathers.

CANON MORAN. Of course I'd like to meet him.

Very loudly, the sound of the flow of the river, tumbling over a waterfall. It is almost sinister.

It is a few days later. CANON MORAN *is cutting his grass.* DEIRDRE *approaches with coffee cups etc. on a tray. She calls out to her father.*

DEIRDRE. Come and have some coffee.

The mowing ceases. DEIRDRE *arranges the cups etc on a table on the lawn. Her father approaches.*

DEIRDRE. You've been writing your sermon.

CANON MORAN. I broke off to have a think about St Paul.

He sits down, takes a cup and saucer from her.

Thank you, dear. That's lovely.

DEIRDRE. I — I cleared the wardrobe out. Mrs O'Neill has the dresses now. And everything else.

CANON MORAN. It's good of you, Deirdre.

DEIRDRE. Some lovely things.

CANON MORAN. You should have kept —

DEIRDRE (*hastily*). No, no. No.

CANON MORAN. Sometime make your choice of the jewellery. We'll send the rest to Dublin, for the others to share. Not that there's much of any value.

DEIRDRE. I'd like the pearl brooch.

CANON MORAN. Then put it aside.

Silence. DEIRDRE *speaks hesitantly.*

DEIRDRE. Father . . . Father, you know I mentioned Harold?

CANON MORAN. Yes, of course.

DEIRDRE. Could he come and stay with us? Would you mind? Would it be all right?

CANON MORAN. Of course I wouldn't mind. I'd be delighted.

DEIRDRE. He's in London. But if I wrote he'd come immediately.

CANON MORAN. Then you must write, my dear.

Fade up very lightly, the Schubert as a background to CANON
MORAN's *voice, in bed, at night.*

CANON MORAN. I can't tell you what it's like having her back at the
    rectory. She seems so happy, all the time. Picking the grapes and
    cooking and cleaning. Remember how we thought she was lost for
    ever? When no letters ever came, no word at all from her? It's a
    miracle that she's back.

Fade up the mooing of the CANON's *single cow as he drives her
from the paddock into the yard at the back of the rectory, and then
into the cowshed, where he proceeds to milk her. His bucket clatters
on the stone floor; milk squirts into it.*

CANON MORAN. Good girl, good girl.

    DEIRDRE *calls out, entering the yard from the house.*

DEIRDRE. Father!

CANON MORAN. I'm here in the cowshed.

    DEIRDRE's *and* HAROLD's *footsteps approach.*

DEIRDRE. Father, this is Harold.

    CANON MORAN *ceases his milking, stands up.*

CANON MORAN. How d'you do?

HAROLD. I'm fine.

CANON MORAN. You've had a good journey, Harold?

HAROLD. Lousy, 'smatter of fact, Mr Moran.

CANON MORAN. Oh, that's too bad.

    There is an awkward silence.

CANON MORAN. Well, I'd better get on with this.

    He milks again.

DEIRDRE. *We'll* get the supper. You sit down in the drawing-room
    with the *Irish Times* when you've finished your milking.

HAROLD. Yeah, you do that, Mr Moran.

    Fade sounds of cow shed.

CANON MORAN. He's not at all like what I expected. He's thin,
    with a thin face that has a birthmark on it, and mouse-coloured hair
    cut very short, cropped almost, and a black leather jacket. Not at
    all like John or Thomas or Carley. They hold hands, and I don't
    remember Linda holding John's much, or Emma Thomas's, or

Una Carley's. He didn't smile. His birthmark's like a scarlet map on his left cheek, like the toe of Italy. Poor fellow! you think when you look at it — and yet a birthmark's much less to bear than other afflictions . . .

The drawing-room.

HAROLD. It's all ready now, Mr Moran.

A rattle of the 'Irish Times' as CANON MORAN *puts it aside.*

CANON MORAN. Thank you, Harold.

They move together from the drawing-room. In the dining-room DEIRDRE *arranges the supper on the table.*

CANON MORAN. For what we're about to receive, may the Lord make us truly thankful.

They sit down. In silence DEIRDRE *doles out the bacon and eggs. Plates are passed, tea poured.*

CANON MORAN. Well, then, what do you think of Co Wexford?

HAROLD. Great, Mr Moran. Really great.

DEIRDRE. Harold's fascinated actually. By Ireland.

HAROLD. The struggle of the Irish people.

CANON MORAN. I — I beg your pardon?

DEIRDRE. It's that that fascinated Harold.

Silence. DEIRDRE *waits for* HAROLD *to say something. When he doesn't she continues herself.*

I didn't know anything about Irish history. I mean not anything that made sense. It was Harold who got me going.

CANON MORAN (*to* HAROLD). Well, that's most interesting. Actually, I've always found Irish history particularly intriguing myself. There's a good story to it, isn't there? Its tragedy's tidily uncomplicated.

This elicits no response. There's another silence.

You've come at a particularly lovely time of year. This countryside's —

DEIRDRE. Actually, Harold doesn't go in for anything like that.

HAROLD. I began to read up on it, Mr Moran: the struggle of the Irish people. 1169 and all that.

CANON MORAN. Yes, I suppose it did all begin then.

HAROLD. No way it didn't, Mr Moran.

CANON MORAN. I see.

HAROLD. Then again that Earl of Essex. The blooming nerve!

CANON MORAN. Yes, I suppose —

HAROLD. Then again the plantations. Then again the Mitchelstown
   Martyrs. The death of Robert Emmet, Sarsfield betrayed, Parnell
   betrayed, Pearse, de Valera. It hasn't been written, Mr Moran,
   the struggle of the Irish people.

CANON MORAN (*mildly*). There's quite a lot actually —

HAROLD. No way's it been written. No way's it finished either. The
   struggle's going on, Mr Moran, until the four green fields of
   Ireland are joined together, like they belong.

DEIRDRE. Harold's read an awful lot actually. Everything he could
   get his hands on.

CANON MORAN. Have you always been interested? Or was it —
   was it meeting Deirdre?

   HAROLD *deliberately doesn't reply.* DEIRDRE *is on the point of
   contributing something but* HAROLD *interrupts by asking a
   question of his own, addressing* CANON MORAN.

DEIRDRE. Well —

HAROLD. D'you know England, Mr Moran?

CANON MORAN. Hardly at all I'm afraid. I've only been in England
   twice in my life. My wife and I went to Gloucestershire once, and
   then again —

HAROLD. Better off without it. A degenerate place, Mr Moran.
   Degraded by class-consciousness on top of the unjust distribution
   of wealth. Take Nottingham where I come from myself. D'you
   know Nottingham, Mr Moran?

CANON MORAN. No. As I —

HAROLD. Better not. Nottingham's the epitomy. (*Pause.*) I'm an
   electrician, Mr Moran, and I'll tell you this: the Midlands of
   England's run on greed. England's heartland they call it. My God!

CANON MORAN. I've read of course — D.H. Lawrence wrote of
   Nottingham —

HAROLD. No better'n a lackey. What's England today. Mr Moran?
   Motorways. Bureaucracy. The Royal Family. You could keep
   an Indian village on what those corgis eat. You could house five
   thousand homeless in Buckingham Palace.

CANON MORAN. On the other hand —

HAROLD. There isn't no other hand, Mr Moran. No way there is.
   Listen: there's brainwashing by television and the newspaper
   barons. No ordinary person has a chance because pap is fed to the

ordinary person. That's a deliberate policy, going back into Victorian times.

CANON MORAN. Oh, but surely —

HAROLD. The time when education and religion were geared to the enslavement of minds. The English people brought it on themselves. They lost their bloody spunk.

DEIRDRE. Harold —

HAROLD. Sorry Mr Moran. Sorry to come out with 'bloody' like that. Only you can't help getting carried off. What I mean is, if England settles for consumer durables what better can you expect? Look at it another way, what better can you expect after the empire the bosses ran? Makes you sick.

CANON MORAN. Well, of course there's been injustice in the past, and no doubt there still is. But actually I rather like the Royal Family.

HAROLD. Take Germany. There's developments taking place underneath the surface there. I mean, it's not what it looks like.

CANON MORAN. Germany?

HAROLD. The status quo'll be turned on its head, if you get what I mean. When the revolution gets a grip anywhere it'll be Germany first of all. And England not long after.

CANON MORAN. Lots of the qualities you dislike so about England apply in Ireland also. I don't know anything very much about newspaper barons, but we have consumer durables and television here too.

HAROLD. England makes me sick.

DEIRDRE *bustles about, gathering up dishes, knives and forks.*

DEIRDRE. No, no, Father. We'll do all this.

Fade out.

Later, in his bedroom, CANON MORAN *prays by the side of his bed before settling down for the night.*

CANON MORAN. . . . who trespass against us. For Thine is the Kingdom, the Power and the Glory. For ever and ever. Amen.

He clambers to his feet, gets into bed, clicks out the light.

CANON MORAN (*whispering*). Goodnight, my dear. Goodnight.

In the garden.
SLATTERY's *post van skids to a halt on the drive.*

SLATTERY. Good morning, Canon. Isn't it keeping up well?

CANON MORAN (*approaching*). It is indeed.

  He takes his letters and the paper.

SLATTERY. I'm bringing you bad news again.

CANON MORAN. Oh?

SLATTERY. It's on your paper there. Two girls. No more than kids, God help them. Will it ever stop, Canon?

CANON MORAN. It sometimes seems it won't.

SLATTERY. Well anyway, I have a couple of trout for you. Fresh as young daisies.

CANON MORAN. Oh, now, that's very kind of you, Slattery.

SLATTERY. Ah sure, I'd only be throwing them away. Good morning to you so, Canon.

  He lets the clutch in. The van speeds off.
  Fade.

In the kitchen pop music comes from the wireless.

DEIRDRE. Good morning, Father.

  She turns the radio off.

CANON MORAN. Ah. Good morning. Good morning, Harold. Did you sleep well?

HAROLD. Lousy, 'smatter of fact, Mr Moran.

DEIRDRE. It's the quietness. I was saying to Harold, you get used to sleeping with a noise and when it isn't there —

HAROLD. So the struggle continues.

CANON MORAN. Well, I —

  HAROLD *laughs.*

HAROLD. I like the way they put it on your newspaper. As good as the *Express* that is. One-sided, I'd say that was.

CANON MORAN. Actually, the *Irish Times* takes a fairly independent line.

HAROLD. I wouldn't want to argue with you, Mr Moran.

CANON MORAN. Slattery brought us some trout.

DEIRDRE. Oh, lovely!

HAROLD. Another aspect of the same thing: she's showing me Kinsella's Barn this afternoon.

CANON MORAN. Kinsella's barn?

DEIRDRE. Harold's interested.

CANON MORAN. Interested?

HAROLD. As I see it, Mr Moran, twelve men and women were marched through Boharbawn to that place. Tied together on the same rope.

CANON MORAN. Well, tied together certainly. But it's — it's a long time ago.

HAROLD. 1798. March fourteen.

CANON MORAN. March fourteen . . .

HAROLD. I've read a thing or two on it. That Sergeant James in command: he led them through the village, with a band playing, am I right in that? An act of education could you call it? An example to the inhabitants of Boharbawn and the country people around? Was that the trick he was up to? 'Don't harbour insurgents, like this lot did. Don't harbour insurgents or you'll end up fried to a frazzle in Kinsella's Barn, with a band playing'. That's about it, isn't it?

CANON MORAN. Yes, that's about it. But there's nothing much to see at Kinsella's Barn. Just the ruin of a wall's all that's left.

HAROLD. Twelve people like in a chain gang. Seven miles he walked them, with the band playing. Just to set them on fire. It's peculiar more people don't come to pay their respects: I was surprised when Deirdre said they didn't.

CANON MORAN. No one goes near the place. It's all best forgotten, you know.

HAROLD. I wouldn't say it was, Mr Moran. I wouldn't say that at all.

Fade.

Later, in the drawing-room, CANON MORAN *attempts to converse with Frances.*

CANON MORAN. He frightens me, Frances. There's something awful in his eyes and his afflicted face. There's cruelty there somewhere, I'm sure of it. *Why* is he so fascinated about a country that isn't his own? *Why* does he refer to 'Ireland's struggle' as if it particularly concerns him? Plans for atrocities fill his mind, I'm sure they do; yet Deirdre loves him. You said it was our blessing that Emma brought Thomas to the rectory, that Linda brought John, that Una eventually brought Carley . . . But Harold hasn't come for a blessing, not to the rectory or to Ireland. Oh my dear, how I wish I could hear you telling me not to be uncharitable.

Silence.

The drawing-room at night.

HAROLD. He was a Nottingham man, you know.

CANON MORAN. Nottingham?

HAROLD. That guy responsible for the burning in Kinsella's Barn.
A soldier of fortune who didn't care what he did. Did you know
Sergeant James acquired great wealth, Mr Moran?

CANON MORAN. No, I wasn't aware of that.

DEIRDRE. Harold found out about him.

HAROLD. He used to boast he was responsible for the death of a
thousand Irish people. It was in Boharbawn he reached the thousand.
They rewarded him well for that.

CANON MORAN. Not much is known about Sergeant James. Just the
legend of Kinsella's Barn.

HAROLD. No way's it a legend.

CANON MORAN. What I —

HAROLD. Know what I mean, you'd feel sick? You'd stand there
looking at that wall with the ivy on it, and you'd feel a revulsion
in your stomach. The band playing, and the bodies alight . . .

CANON MORAN. What I mean is that it has all passed into local legend.
No one doubts it took place of course, there's no question about
that. But two centuries have almost passed.

HAROLD. And nothing has changed. The Irish people still share their
bondage with the twelve in Kinsella's Barn.

CANON MORAN. Round here of course —

HAROLD. It's not round here that matters, Mr Moran. The struggle's
world wide, the sickness's everywhere actually. At least Kinsella
got his chips. At least that's something.

CANON MORAN. Oh no, no. That poor man was totally innocent.

HAROLD (*sharply*). His own labourers hanged him.

CANON MORAN. But they shouldn't have, Harold. That's part of the
tragedy also. His barn was used for that horrible purpose just
because it was big enough and convenient. There were heavy
stones nearby that could be piled up against the door. The soldiers
worked all that out.

HAROLD *gives a little disbelieving laugh.*

Kinsella was miles away that day. Ditching a field.

HAROLD. It's too long ago to know where he was. And if he was keeping a low profile in a ditch it would have been by arrangement with the imperial forces.

CANON MORAN. Oh no, no, no, Harold. It was terrible that they hanged poor Kinsella, an awful example of vengeance. They turned on him for no reason whatsoever. It was as bad as the conflagration itself.

HAROLD. I wouldn't agree with you, Mr Moran. Though I grant you, of course he wasn't in the same class as this Sergeant James. When you look at Ireland today, Mr Moran, it's the Sergeant Jameses you have to remember. Butchering for profit.

DEIRDRE. Goodnight, Father.

CANON MORAN. What? Oh, good night, dear.

HAROLD. Night, Mr Moran.

Fade.

In the bedroom.

CANON MORAN. Is he mad? He's an Englishman, and yet he hates his own country. So much that he espouses a foreign cause in order to damage it. You read about such Englishmen: men from Ealing and Liverpool and Wolverhampton who even change their names to Irish names, who even learn the Irish language in order to ingratiate with the new Irish revolutionaries? Is that what Harold is, Frances? Has he come here to make the most of Ireland's troubles? (*Becoming emotional and terrified.*) Why *are* they here? Why have both of them come to Ireland? (*A long pause. He calms down, speaks quietly now.*) You'd know. You'd tell me. Is he the same kind of person as Sergeant James? Has he come here to deal in death and destruction? It doesn't matter that they seem to be on different sides. He's merciless, like Sergeant James was. You'd say the same, I'm sure you would, my dear. He *loves* the thought of an innocent farmer being put to death, as that monstrous man loved the thought of those innocent people burning like straw. Sergeant James had an affliction also, a humped back, a withered arm. He ravaged a country that existed for its spoils, and his crime is still at hand so that another Englishman can make matters worse by attempting to make amends. Our daughter has brought him here to find inspiration in Kinsella's Barn. They have journeyed to it as journeys are made to holy places. (*Becoming agitated.*) Isn't that the truth? Isn't it, Frances? Isn't it?

Silence.

(*More calmly*.) How could I ever have felt suspicious of the others, Thomas's smile, good-natured smile, John's little moustache, Carley's flushed cheeks? Yet I hated the thought of any one of them embracing our daughters or even touching them. (*Pause*.) I hoped this afternoon they would quarrel on their walk; that they wouldn't speak when they returned, that Harold would simply go away. (*Pause*.) His fingernails are edged with black. (*Pause*.) I *prayed* they might quarrel on their walk. Deirdre turned her back on us: what could be expected when she returns to the rectory with a man? (*Vehemently, bitterly*.) Would Emma or Linda or Una wear clothes that don't seem clean or become involved with wickedness? (*Almost weeping*.) Oh, why can you not answer? Why can you not speak?

Silence.

The congregation at CANON MORAN's *church sing the last verse of Hymn 421.* CANON MORAN *mounts the pulpit steps. The hymn comes to an end; the congregation sit down.*

CANON MORAN. St Luke 15, verse 32 . . . *for this thy brother was dead, and is alive again; and was lost and is found.* (*Pause*.) Repentance. (*Pause*.) And fear. The awful fear of being in the dark, of not knowing . . .

The sound of the burning of Kinsella's Barn, the uneasy neighing of the soldiers' horses, the screaming, the band. The sound of the fire reaches a crescendo, begins to fade.
    HAROLD *and* DEIRDRE's *voices are heard over the fire.*

HAROLD. Seven miles he walked them with the band playing. Just to set them on fire.

DEIRDRE. I have a friend. Someone who's been good to me.

HAROLD. The struggle of the Irish people. I began to read up on it, Mr Moran.

DEIRDRE. Harold's fascinated actually.

HAROLD. Then again that Earl of Essex. The blooming nerve!

The voices of DEIRDRE *and* HAROLD *become fragmented and jumbled as they repeat, over and over again, these statements. The sound of the fire and the screaming and the band grows louder until the voices are lost.*
In church, CANON MORAN *has lost his way in his sermon. His parishioners shuffle uneasily. He speaks falteringly.*

CANON MORAN. Evil . . . evil . . . evil drains people of their humour

and their compassion. People pretend even to themselves. Kinsella
was innocent of everything. He should never have been murdered
also. Suffering and destruction are never inflicted for any reason that
can possibly be good.

*There is a ripple of astonishment among the small congregation.
CANON MORAN's words have come from nowhere and do not
make sense.*

CANON MORAN. And now to God the Father, God the Son, God the
Holy Ghost . . .

The congregation stands.

CANON MORAN. Hymn 450. 'Come, Holy Spirit, calm our minds.'

*The congregation sings.
In the porch, CANON MORAN shakes hands with his parishioners.*

Are you well again, Mrs Davis?

MRS DAVIS. Not too bad, Canon. Not too bad, thank you.

MR WILLOUGHBY. Goodbye so, Canon. You're still managing all
right?

CANON MORAN. Oh, I am, I am. Thank you, Mr Willoughby.

MRS O'NEILL. Deirdre's still with you, is she, Canon?

CANON MORAN. Ah, she is, yes.

MRS O'NEILL. Well, that's great company, isn't it?

Car doors bang, bicycles are mounted.

The dining-room. Sunday lunch.

DEIRDRE. We'll probably go tomorrow.

CANON MORAN. Go?

DEIRDRE. We'll probably take the Dublin bus.

HAROLD. I'd like to see Dublin.

CANON MORAN. And then you're returning to London?

HAROLD. We're easy about that. (*Pause.*) I'm a tradesman, Mr Moran,
an electrician.

CANON MORAN. I know you're an electrician, Harold.

HAROLD. What I mean is I'm on my own. I'm not answerable to the
bosses. There's always a bob or two waiting in London.

CANON MORAN. I'm sorry, I — I —

DEIRDRE. What Harold means is he can stay over here as long as he likes. It won't be difficult to pick up work when he returns.

CANON MORAN. I see.

HAROLD. Look around a bit, we thought.

CANON MORAN. You're not going up to the North?

DEIRDRE. Well, we might go anywhere —

HAROLD. Yeah, we might go anywhere.

CANON MORAN. But the North: surely there's not much there to —

HAROLD. There might be. There might be plenty to interest us,
Mr Moran. (*Pause*.) But first of all I'd like to meet the Dublin
people.

CANON MORAN (*alarmed*). What people?

HAROLD (*smoothly*). Just anyone, Mr Moran. Just anyone at all.

> *The eat in silence.*
> *Fade.*

Fade up country sounds: DEIRDRE *and her father go on their last
walk together.*

DEIRDRE. It was good of you to have us. We've enjoyed it, Father.

CANON MORAN. It's been nice, Deirdre.

DEIRDRE. I'll write more often.

CANON MORAN. I wish you could have seen your mother again. I
wish she were here now.

DEIRDRE. I know.

CANON MORAN. I keep wanting her to be a ghost. I feel she'll talk to
me then.

DEIRDRE (*gently*). It'll take a little time.

> *They walk on. There's silence between them for a moment.*

CANON MORAN. He was just a farmer, you know. Kinsella.

> *This surprises* DEIRDRE. *She imagines he's wandering a bit, and
> gently she reminds him.*

DEIRDRE. It was Mother we were talking about.

CANON MORAN. Yes, I know. (*After a pause*.) Is — Is Harold —

DEIRDRE. Is Harold what, Father?

CANON MORAN. Why's he so interested in Ireland, Deirdre?

DEIRDRE. English people sometimes are. He likes it, I suppose.

CANON MORAN. I wouldn't take him up to the North.

DEIRDRE (*laughing*). Oh, you never know with Harold. He goes where the fancy takes him, you know. I'll give everything a good clean-over before we go. Keep you going for a bit.

Fade.

The sound of a vacuum cleaner, DEIRDRE humming as she works. Outside the rectory, HAROLD bangs the door of the car, having deposited his and DEIRDRE's suitcases. The vacuum cleaner can still be heard in the background.
CANON MORAN's footsteps on the gravel.

CANON MORAN. I thought there might be a pound or two of grapes ready.

HAROLD. Grapes, Mr Moran?

CANON MORAN. To drop off in Enniscorthy. But there's nothing ripe.

HAROLD. Deirdre and I had a few yesterday.

CANON MORAN. You're very welcome.

Silence.

HAROLD. Thanks a ton, Mr Moran. Thanks a ton for everything.

CANON MORAN. Well . . .

HAROLD. She told me about the barn. Nine months ago maybe. In the pub one night. We were sitting there and then she told me. Right out of the blue. It was that got me interested.

CANON MORAN. I see.

HAROLD. She wants to leave the place trim for you.

CANON MORAN. Yes, I know.

HAROLD. She likes to clean, does Deirdre.

CANON MORAN. Yes, I shouldn't go up to the North, Harold. It's not — it's different from down here.

HAROLD. Oh well, we'll see (*Pause.*) She got up really early, you know. She had the vacuum going at six.

CANON MORAN. It's very kind of Deirdre.

HAROLD. You're fond of her, aren't you, Mr Moran?

CANON MORAN does not reply immediately.

CANON MORAN. Yes. Yes, very fond. I think it's time we were off.

He opens one of the car doors, hoots the horn.

HAROLD. It's just there's places up there I wouldn't mind seeing. Know what I mean, Mr Moran?

The vacuum cleaner stops.

CANON MORAN. Yes. Yes, of course.

HAROLD. Cheers for everything again, Mr Moran. I'll keep an eye on her for you.

HAROLD gets into the car, bangs the door behind him. DEIRDRE emerges from the rectory, banging the hall door behind her.

DEIRDRE. I've done everything I could think of.

CANON MORAN. We'd best be off.

The car crunches over the gravel.

SLATTERY's post van speeds on a road too narrow for speeding. He hears a horn, applies the brakes, skilfully backs into a gateway. CANON MORAN's Vauxhall approaches round a bend. SLATTERY addresses the clergyman through the two open windows.

SLATTERY. Did you catch it, Canon?

CANON MORAN. We caught it. Plenty of time.

SLATTERY. Well, it'll be quiet for you now.

CANON MORAN. Yes, it will.

SLATTERY. I'll maybe have another fish on Wednesday.

CANON MORAN. Oh now, you mustn't —

SLATTERY. Ah, why wouldn't I slip it along to you, Canon? Cheerio then.

The Vauxhall crawls past the van, then increases its speed and eventually turns in at the rectory gates.

CANON MORAN hears again the burning of the barn, the uneasiness of the soldiers' horses, the screaming, the band, and then HAROLD's voice.

HAROLD'S VOICE. So the struggle continues.

The noise of burning, screaming, etc. It becomes confused, emerges into clarity again with the sound of explosions, sporadic gunfire, the whine of ambulances, the shouting on a Belfast street. It ceases abruptly.

DEIRDRE'S VOICE. Harold's fascinated actually.

The car has come to a stop in front of the rectory. CANON MORAN gets out, crosses the gravel to the seat on the lawn. He sits down with a sigh.

CANON MORAN. You should come now. You should cross the gravel and the lawn with our two cups of coffee on a tray, and I'd tell you that they caught the bus with twenty minutes to spare. 'Funny little Deirdre', you'd probably say, and then you'd laugh at me for being so ridiculous. (*Pause.*) But I know it's only a trick of the autumn sunshine, no more than pretence that you sit down beside me.

Very faintly — much more faintly than we've heard it before — Frances plays the Schubert piece.

'Harold's just a talker': is that what you would say? 'Not at all like Sergeant James.' Between them they've blurred your fingerprints away to nothing. 'Harold's just a talker': I swear I can hear you. Of course it isn't a trick of the autumn sunshine: you're there on the gravel and the lawn, you're here beside me. They've made a ghost of you; at last I can hear your voice. (*A long pause, while he listens.*) No. No, don't say anything else. (*Becoming upset.*) No, please don't say anything else.

Music, becoming very loud, continues for some time. The music cuts out abruptly.

A radio plays.

NEWSCASTER. . . . . the death of the third hunger-striker. The children — according to reports which have not yet been confirmed — were caught in the crossfire as further shots were exchanged. But the organisers of the protest insist that no weapons were carried by their supporters. Reports are still coming in, and further details concerning the deaths of the children will be given when the situation has clarified. (*Pause.*) The price of petrol is likely to be increased following the decision of the . . .

CANON MORAN *turns off the radio.*
The Schubert piece plays very faintly.
CANON MORAN *whispers through it.*

CANON MORAN. I wish you'd said Harold was just a talker and left it at that. What's the *good* of saying he's right? (*His voice rises agitatedly.*) What comfort's there in it? Why did you always have to tell what you thought to be the truth? (*Becoming very emotional.*) He's a horrible kind of person. You're not here, you didn't meet him. Can't you see he's a horrible kind of person. How could a person like that possibly be right?

The Schubert continues.